SELF
PARENTING

SELF PARENTING

THE COMPLETE GUIDE TO YOUR INNER CONVERSATIONS

Dr. John K. Pollard, III

Illustrations by Linda Nusbaum

Generic Human Studies Publishing
Malibu, California

This book is dedicated to the memory and works of
Max Freedom Long.

It is my sincere desire that *Self-Parenting* will
inspire and teach others as much as his amazing
discoveries have inspired, and continue
to inspire, me.

Published by
Generic Human Studies Publishing
28128 Pacific Coast Highway, Suite 161
P.O. Box 6466, Malibu, CA 90265

Design by Words & Deeds, Los Angeles

Printed in the United States of America

Library of Congress Cataloging-in-Publication Data

Pollard, John K., 1950–
    Self-parenting : the complete guide to your inner
conversations.

    Bibliography: p.
    1. Happiness. 2. Self-perception. 3. Imaginary
conversations. 4. Problem-solving—Problems, exercises, etc.
5. Self-perception—Problems, exercises, etc.
I. Title
BF575.H27P65   1987   158'.1   86-83037
ISBN 0-942055-25-X (pbk.)

ACKNOWLEDGMENTS

I have many thanks to give:

— to Michael Hesse who made the first introductions in 1969 and taught me so much;

— to Maryann Ridini and Bro Half for editorial advice and the reassuring guidance of professionals from the start;

— to Greg Stanley for his amazing Whitehall Seminar and our many late night conversations in which he inspired, encouraged, and empowered me to follow my dream;

— to my staff and patients at F.C.C., whose support and dedication enabled me to research and write;

— to Tim Pailing, without whose friendship I wouldn't have been able to complete this project;

— to Ralph Strauch, for advice and support on the Mac, as well as outstanding Feldenkrais treatments;

— to Australia and its people:
  — Di Searle, a Living Goddess, who made this book especially accessible to all;
  — Peter & Judy Derig whose love, support, and nurturing, was so freely given and is so deeply appreciated;

— the Sydney kids, Angela Thornton and her cute friend, for being the first to see the light, as well as organizing and co-teaching the first Self-Parenting Trainings;

— to Linda Cobb and Judi Andersen for their insightful advice, editing, feedback, and support back in the U.S.A;

— to Dan Poynter, Linda Nusbaum and Suzette Mahr for their highly conscious "real world" contributions and brilliant support launching this effort;

— to the last and the best, Meredith Paton, who was always there waiting and for whose quality of love I've been holding out for longer than I care to remember.

To all of the above and more, thank you; there is so much yet to come.

CONTENTS

Part III
THE SELF-PARENTING EXERCISES

INTRODUCTION

Each of us Self-Parents within our mind all the time. We may not be aware of it, but this doesn't change the fact that we do. Self-Parenting is a natural component of our thoughts, emotions, and behaviors in life. Daily, we make Self-Parenting decisions that reflect the way our Inner Parent and Inner Child voices combine in our mind to interact with our environment. By becoming more aware of the way we Self-Parent within our Inner Conversations, we can start to make conscious choices in our lives rather than acting by default.

Self-Parenting: The Complete Guide to Your Inner Conversations is divided into three sections to facilitate understanding of the fundamental concepts of positive Self-Parenting.

Part One introduces you to your Inner Conversations. These four chapters introduce and describe the voices of the Inner Parent and the Inner Child as well as show how these voices interact within the Inner Conversations of your mind. Becoming aware of your Inner Conversations initiates Level One, or intellectual, understanding of the Self-Parenting process.

Part Two introduces you to your Inner Conflicts. Inner Conflicts occur between the needs of your Inner Parent and Inner Child within your Inner Conversations. Practical examples and steps show you how to resolve Inner Conflicts with the positive Win/Win solution. Experiencing the source of your Inner Conflicts initiates Level Two, or emotional, understanding of the Self-Parenting process.

Part Three introduces you to the Self-Parenting Exercises. By practicing half-hour sessions in the prescribed manner, you will experience many positive benefits in your life. Designed as a workbook, this section provides many examples and practical uses for your Self-Parenting sessions to facilitate Self-Parenting in the "real world." Learning and practicing the half-hour sessions initiates Level Three, or practical, understanding of the Self-Parenting process.

As each section builds on the previous section, it is recommended that time and care be taken to thoroughly understand each section of **Self-Parenting: The Complete Guide To Your Inner Conversations** before going to the next. In this way your Self-Parenting sessions will have the greatest opportunity for success.

PART I
YOUR INNER CONVERSATIONS

HAVE YOU EVER HEARD A CONVERSATION IN YOUR MIND?

Have you ever heard a conversation in your mind?

If you think you have, think you haven't, or if you are saying to yourself right now:

"Well, I'm not sure if I ever have heard a conversation in my mind..."

...then stop, take a minute, and listen; you might just be hearing an internal dialogue that sounds something like this:

INNER CONVERSATION:
While reading this book

A: "Me? A conversation in my mind?
What does that mean?"

> **B:** "I don't know, but I don't think I
> should be having conversations
> in my mind."

A: "Maybe it's when you hear voices."

> **B:** "No way! I can't tell anybody that I
> hear voices in my head. They'll
> think I'm crazy."

A: "Well, maybe, but there is some kind of
conversation going on in there. I think a lot."

> **B:** "I don't know. Maybe once I
> talked to myself."

A: "I think I do hear conversations in my mind,
come to think of it."

> **B:** "Yeah, I guess you could say that."

A: "What kind of book is this anyway?"

> **B:** "I don't know, but I want to
> find out."

A: "Me too."

> **B:** "So, keep reading and see
> what happens."

A: "Okay!"

There are conversations going on inside your mind all the time. They are very **deep**, very **subtle**, and the exchanges happen very quickly. Inner Conversations occur much more quickly than any ordinary conversation between two people.

At first, when introduced to the concept of your Inner Conversations, you may not believe they even exist. This is because they take place below the surface level of your awareness. Once you become aware of their existence, however, you will start to hear some of the louder Inner Conversations going on inside your mind. After a short period of time the presence of your Inner Conversations will become very familiar to you.

Once you start
listening carefully to your
Inner Conversations and
begin using the Self-
Parenting exercises in this
guide, you will hear them
throughout all your waking
activities.

They occur while
you are reading, making
love, eating dinner, watch-
ing television, riding in the car, walking your dog,
sunning at the beach, or during any other activity you
can name.

Inner Conversations also take place in your mind when you are riding a bike, planning a vacation, bowling, going to school, hiking in the mountains, or jogging in Central Park. (I can hear that one right now!)

They occur on first dates, second dates, and all following dates. Inner Conversations do not mysteriously disappear the moment you turn eighteen, twenty-one, forty, or even sixty for that matter. They are a daily, weekly, and monthly staple of your emotional/mental diet. Certain Inner Conversations with specific themes can be repeated and continued for years if the circumstances surrounding them are not resolved.

This Self-Parenting guide outlines many typical examples of Inner Conversations recorded by students during half-hour sessions called "Self-Parenting Exercises." These half-hour sessions will enable you to recognize these mental discussions and teach you how to understand and use your own Inner Conversations to Self-Parent in a positive way.

ere is an example of a simple **Inner Conversation** that you might have had once or twice after work or school:

INNER CONVERSATION:
A single adult around six o'clock,
after work or school.

A: "What shall we do for dinner?"

        B: "I don't know."

A: "Well, you better have something to eat or
you'll pass out."

        B: "Peanut butter sandwiches."

A: "Don't be ridiculous, that's what
we had for lunch."

        B: "I'm not hungry then."

A: "Yeah, but you will be. There's nothing
in the fridge."

        B. "Let's go to the store."

A: "I'd like to but there's no time. We've
got to leave at seven o'clock for
that lecture on Self-Parenting."

        B: "Let's stop at McDonald's
on the way."

A: "We did that yesterday and the day before."

        B: "How about Burger King,
it's real close!"

A: "Okay, sounds good..."

Always remember that your Inner Conversations happen almost subconsciously—as if on automatic pilot.

nner Conversations also occur with more intensity during more stressful life situations such as the following:

INNER CONVERSATION:
A worried mother whose daughter hasn't come home at eleven o'clock when she said she would.

A: "Oh god! Where's my baby?"

B: "Don't worry. She'll be fine."

A: "But it's 11:30 and she's not home yet."

B: "She's probably just having fun and forgot the time."

A: "What if she's hurt?"

> **B**: "You worry too much,
> she'll be home any minute now."

A: "If my baby is hurt I'll never
forgive myself."

> **B**: "She's a good girl and if
> anything happens she'll call
> and let us know."

A: "I'm going to call Suzie's mother
to see if she's over there."

> B: "Now you're starting to
> sound like a Frantic Fran."

A: "I am a Frantic Fran, give me a break!"

> **B**: "At least wait another half-hour."

A: "Maybe I should call the police."

> **B**: "Maybe you should calm down."
> (The phone rings!)

A: "Oh my god, what if that's the hospital."

> **B**: "Phew, maybe now we can
> find out what's going on and
> calm down for a while."

A: "What if it's not her?"

> **B**: "Answer the phone. It's
> rung twice already."

Don't these Inner Conversations sound familiar?

Aren't they typical of the kinds of thoughts that might run through your mind in similar situations? Most people aren't consciously aware of their Inner Conversations. They simply don't think about them because they occur so naturally.

Outer conversations between people are easy to study and understand, since they occur in the outer physical world. They can be recorded, written down, and then analyzed.

Your Inner Conversations on the other hand are much more difficult to study carefully. They occur mentally inside your mind and can't be recorded, even though their existence is just as real.

Learning more about your Inner Conversations can help you in many ways. Your Inner Conversations are the key to your true thoughts and feelings. Since you must know what you want in order to get it, your Inner Conversations will tell you, in the most direct way possible, exactly what you are thinking and feeling so that you can get exactly what you want.

The first step to positive Self-Parenting is to train your conscious awareness to listen to the the specific types of Inner Conversations that only you have. By practicing and using the Self-Parenting Exercises found in Part III, you will develop a deep sensitivity to and awareness of your Inner Conversations. You will learn methods to record your Inner Conversations so you may study and improve your Self-Parenting. You will also learn to use these half-hour sessions to easily resolve any Inner Conflicts that develop in your mind.

Studying your Inner Conversations can also reveal the concealed barriers to your personal happiness! Every emotional/mental problem you have in life takes place initially as a conflict within your Inner Conversations. Whether you are afraid, bored, confused, or angry, your Inner Conversations are telling you something: what you need to do next to improve your life, to make it easier or better. The more you learn to positively Self-Parent your Inner Conversations, the more meaningful your life will become.

Your Inner Conversations: Who Are the Participants?

For there to be a conversation inside your mind, it must occur between two points of view. If only one voice existed in your mind it wouldn't have anyone else to talk to or respond to it.

These two voices are called the Inner Parent and the Inner Child. They have amazingly different personalities and characteristics.

When you were young
you absorbed and internalized the
personalities of your father and
mother (or their equivalent roles).
You were biologically programmed to model and mimic them by
the age of seven as part of the
normal process of human
development. As a result, you
unconsciously absorbed your
parents' ideas, viewpoints, and
mannerisms.

These attitudes and
opinions became
the voice for one
side of your mental
Inner Conversation:
the **Inner Parent.**

As a child you also had your own pint-sized ego and outlook on life. You judged and formed a set of opinions and reactions to your parents and the world around you. Right or wrong you made decisions about the way things were in the world and these were also recorded in your mind.

Today this voice still reacts within you the same way as when you were young—even though your childhood might have been twenty, forty, or sixty years ago. This voice is called the **Inner Child.**

Your Inner Conversations are the dialogue between these two different voices. These two points of view within you also represent the interaction between the rational mind (thinking) and the emotional heart (feeling).

Each voice in your Inner Conversations has a particular style and method of approaching the problems of living. The Inner Parent has its mental opinion, intellectual advice, and rational reasoning. The Inner Child has its emotional feelings, irrational reactions, and subjective responses. Both Selves have needs they feel are important and that they want met.

As you go through life you are confronted with different choices and ways to handle your experiences. You make outer choices based on the two Inner Voices of your mind. Sometimes these voices are in harmony; other times they disagree. The decisions you make and the circumstances in your life are a result of the combined opinions of both Inner Parent and Inner Child as to the best way to Self-Parent yourself.

Frequently your Inner Conversations will reflect disagreement between the two Inner Voices.

These confrontations, called **Inner Conflicts**, take the form of classic outer parent/outer child arguments except they occur within your mind. This is because the types of problems you now experience in your Inner Conversations were first encountered as outer problems while you were growing up.

Outer conflicts you have had with "significant others" such as your parents, grandparents, or other role models are now being repeated inside your mind as Inner Conflicts. They have become internalized versions of your actual outer parent/outer child conflicts which remain unresolved. Positive Self-Parenting will help both voices of your Inner Conversations to meet their needs.

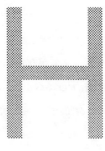ere is another
example of an
Inner Conversation
volunteered by one
of our workshop
participants:

How about another classic **Inner Conversation** culled from the experiences of a thousand outer conversations:

Have you noticed that these Inner Conversations sound just like the outer ones you may have had in the past with your outer parents?

GOOD! The difference is that once you tune into them, you will find those outer conversations with your parents are STILL HAPPENING inside your mind!

They occur even when your parents are not in sight, even if they've been dead for many years. This is because your Inner Conversations continue to influence your life as a mental replay of the teachings and conflicts learned during your childhood.

As you begin listening more and more to your Inner Conversations you will gain more familiarity with these two voices and hear each of them more distinctly. This book will show you how to start opening up your Inner Conversations to more conscious awareness so that you can improve your life and your feelings about yourself immeasurably.

With positive Self-Parenting you will also learn how to resolve Inner Conflicts that are preventing you from experiencing happiness, meaning, and fulfillment in your life. Positive Self-Parenting in your Inner Conversations is the key to your personal happiness.

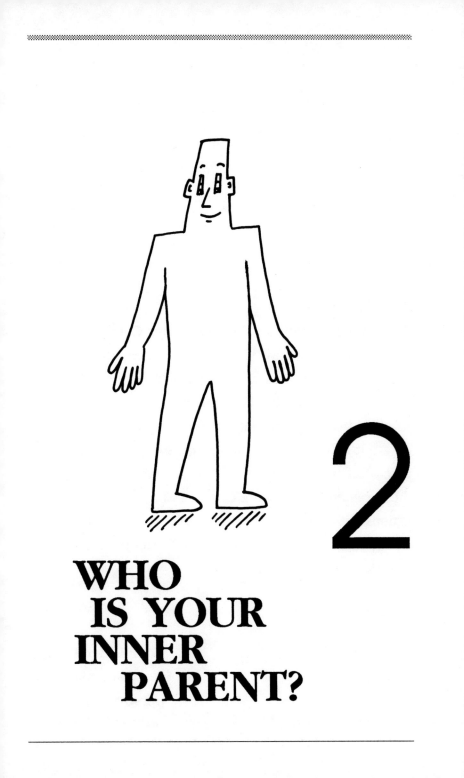

WHO
IS YOUR
INNER
PARENT?

2

One participant in your Inner Conversations guides your daily activities and is actively involved in planning for your future. This voice, called the Inner Parent, results from the individualized parenting you received from your parents (or their substitutes).

It reflects the specific qualities of programming received from your outer parents as well as portions of the experiences you were exposed to through inter-actions with your grandparents, siblings, relatives, peers, teachers, coaches, or religious leaders during your formative years.

Your Inner Parent
is usually called the
personality or **ego**.

It voices all the comments and attitudes your outer parents gave to you about every conceivable aspect of life. When you were young and impressionable you mirrored the style, attitudes and mannerisms of your parents.

You were biologically programmed from birth to mimic your parents' behavior to serve as a model or template to develop your own style of behavior. Watching them was your way of learning how to Self-Parent as an adult.

You start to develop your Inner Parent voice at a very early age! By age two to four, you had already established the psycholog- ical foundation of independence that evolved into your Inner Parent.

When you were born it was as if your mind was a blank computer disk. To help you begin using your new computer, two advanced computers (in the form of your father and mother) began to simultaneously put new information into your data banks.

As a result, your Inner Parent took on many of your outer parents' personality characteristics. For example if your father was emotionally cool and your mother was emotionally warm, your own Inner Parent will have a combination of these two personalities and characteristics. If your grandparents were a big part of your childhood you will also have some of their individual traits in your Inner Parent.

As you began exploring
this strange and wonderful world,
sometimes you would use programming data from one parent and
sometimes the other. You received
further input as you began to interact with other sources of programming around you such as teachers,
television, and peers.

All of these experiences,
conscious and unconscious, helped
you to form the Inner Parent you
have today.

Each person's Inner Parent is unique, reflecting the specific combination of programming only they received. Even children with the same outer parents develop different Inner Parents because each child in a family receives different parenting.

Social and cultural factors also provide a major influence. For example, growing up during the fifties or sixties, as opposed to the seventies or eighties, would distinctly influence the social voice of your Inner Parent. Growing up in Australia, Bali, the United States, Russia or South America would also culturally impact your Inner Parent.

As childhood ends and you gradually assume adult responsibility for your life, the external programming you received as a child is internalized and becomes the Self-Parenting guidance in your life. Now, as an adult, your Inner Parent uses the stored memories of your upbringing to guide and direct your life. Since you absorbed your parental patterns at such an early age, it is easy to take them for granted; however, the combined effect of this programming may be positive, negative, or a combination of both.

The Positive Inner Parent

The potential strengths of your Inner Parent voice are the same strengths that the ideal outer parent would have. Your Inner Parent can be an excellent teacher, providing guidance and setting examples for your Inner Child. Your Inner Parent can maintain an intimate sense of caring and support for your Inner Child so that it may develop its own talents and skills.

When you express positive concern for your Inner Child or give it encouragement you are voicing the positive Inner Parent.

During times of stress the positive Inner Parent is a calming, soothing voice that is always present to help and support your Inner Child. The Inner Parent makes decisions, chooses options, and evaluates importances for both Selves.

The positive Inner Parent will support and nurture the Inner Child when it is scared or angry by asking the Inner Child what it needs and providing it. The positive Inner Parent can provide the Inner Child with whatever it wants or needs by practicing the Self-Parenting Exercises and through positive Self-Parenting within the Inner Conversations.

Training and experience allow the positive Inner Parent to become highly developed in rational thinking and intellectual activity. This is the voice within you that spends a lot of time "figuring things out" with all the consequences and ramifications.

The Inner Parent is also good at making choices which involve complicated issues. It breaks down actions into past, present, and future. It enjoys drawing up boundaries, legal documents, and using facts and figures. Much of our outer communication is derived from the voice of the Inner Parent, especially when we are trying to be polite or formal.

The positive Inner Parent provides stability and support for the Inner Child by being nurturing and loving during Self-Parenting interactions with the Inner Child. Part of this process is achieved by the elimination of negative self-programming. The other part comes from practicing positive Self-Parenting styles within your Inner Conversations, as discussed in Part III.

If your outer parents and significant others did a good job of nurturing you during childhood, you will have a positive, nurturing Inner Parent.

The Negative Inner Parent

The negative Inner Parent is susceptible to the same weaknesses of neglectful and non-nurturing behavior that your outer parents might have used. Your Inner Parent can be quick to judge and lecture your Inner Child. It is common for it to warn, advise, or berate the feelings of the Inner Child.

Many times your Inner Parent will make a major life decision without even asking your Inner Child how it feels, just as your outer parents did to you.

While being rational may be the Inner Parent's strong suit, it can also have some pretty serious programming flaws. In other words it can act very irrationally at times by tying itself (and the Inner Child) up with erroneous thinking. It can be petty and nit-pick unimportant points. It is the "should" side of the Inner Conversation, tending to be the voice that says "you should do this" and "you shouldn't do that." It can also be an overly critical and threatening voice. Many negative traits you were exposed to while being parented are apt to be part of your Self-Parenting.

Your Inner Parent has a major position of influence over your Inner Child and is likely to be the voice that you hear the loudest and the longest in your Inner Conversations.

The biggest test for the Inner Parent comes during an Inner Conflict, when the Inner Parent and Inner Child have an extreme clash of needs. In these circumstances the negative Inner Parent is prone to overpower the Inner Child by virtue of its position of power and authority.

However, when you, as the Inner Parent, win battles of Inner Conflict using your natural power in a negative way, it will be at the expense of your Inner Child. If your Inner Parent does not nurture your Inner Child, the joy and enthusiasm of life will be missing. This plays havoc with the ability of both Inner Selves to be happy.

Have you ever heard new parents say that
they have no intention of making the same mistakes
with their children that their parents made with them?
Later they find themselves repeating verbatim the
words and actions of their own parents. You won't
need your own children to discover that you do this
when Self-Parenting as well. When you begin working
with the Self-Parenting Exercises you will see that you
are still being treated and guided as if by your parents.
Only now you are doing it to yourself, all by yourself,
within your Inner Conversations.

The negative Inner Parent often neglects,
invalidates, misunderstands, or completely ignores the
needs and desires of the Inner Child. It can abuse its
Inner Child by being selfish and demanding, or by
being too much of a perfectionist and putting undue
pressure on the Inner Child.

If your outer parents did a poor job of nurturing and loving you during your childhood, you will
tend toward non-nourishing and negative Self-
Parenting.

The Ideal Role of the Inner Parent

The ideal role of the Inner Parent is to love, support, and nurture the Inner Child. It is able to accept, love, and nurture the Inner Child while still having a sense of the Inner Child being a separate and distinct Self. The ideal Inner Parent does not feel that it "owns" the Inner Child any more than an outer parent should feel that he or she "owns" an outer child.

The ideal Inner Parent uses all the positive generic parent/child interaction skills with a natural ease and knowledge based upon the accumulation of years of intimate, loving, and nurturing interaction.

Another function of the ideal Inner Parent is to guide and encourage the Inner Child through the exploration of its interests and talents. As your Inner Parenting skills improve you can help your Inner Child discover and develop its natural aptitudes and qualities as well as teach your Inner Child about life. By practicing the Self-Parenting Exercises you will create deeper levels of caring and nurturing as you build and maintain higher levels of self-esteem.

The ideal Inner Parent supports the physical, emotional, mental, and social levels of the Inner Child.

The ideal Inner Parent pays attention to and meets the physical needs and desires of the Inner Child by providing an environment of warmth, security, and safety. It takes care of and watches out for the health needs of the Inner Child. It encourages the Inner Child to play through using its body and developing its senses.

The ideal Inner Parent is sensitive to the emotional condition and state of the Inner Child. It demonstrates and shows understanding for the needs, wants, and desires of the Inner Child. It is positive and nurturing when interacting with the Inner Child by being a good communicator. The ideal Inner Parent helps and guides the Inner Child to develop and establish its own independent identity and personality. It also becomes a life-long companion and mentor for the Inner Child.

On the mental level, the ideal Inner Parent teaches the Inner Child about life and provides reasonable explanations for its questions. It encourages, guides, and supports the Inner Child in the discovery of its interests and talents. It willingly and competently accepts the role and responsibilities of positively Self-Parenting the Inner Child.

For example, your ideal, natural, and free- flowing Inner Parent can provide an atmosphere of comfort for your Inner Child by reading this book and practicing the Self-Parenting Exercises. As a result you will start paying more attention to the needs, wants, and desires of your Inner Child and begin to fulfill them. You will become more sensitive to the emotional feelings and overall state of your Inner Child as well as being more positive and nurturing during your Self-Parenting.

The ultimate role or ideal purpose of the Inner Parent is to

LEARN
HOW TO
LOVE,
SUPPORT,
and NURTURE
the INNER CHILD.

This is the key to your personal happiness and fulfillment. To improve your loving and nurturing qualities as an Inner Parent you need only adopt positive outer parenting skills into your Inner Conversations. Once your Inner Parent makes a commitment to this role it will be very effective in Self-Parenting your Inner Child. Best of all, your Inner Parent and Inner Child will love the way you feel.

3

WHO
IS YOUR
INNER
CHILD?

Your Inner Child is a completely separate and distinct Self from your Inner Parent. It represents your feelings, emotions, and reactions to the world. Your Inner Child is the bouncy, bubbly, and happy side of you.

This Inner Voice usually deals with needs or activities that concern the here and now, especially if they might make your Inner Child feel more comfortable or pleasured.

Often your Inner Child cries out for the fulfillment of a physical need or desire.

This voice can be quite insistent and loud. Demands such as, "I'm hungry," "I'm tired," "I'm bored," "I want to go to the beach," "I don't want to go to work." "I don't feel well," "I want..." can often be heard sounding off within you.

Your Inner Child can be very determined and active when it wants something. This is your Inner Conversation's equivalent to the non-stop begging of a child wanting a hug from its mother, or candy at the supermarket.

The characteristics you had as an outer child from birth to age seven are the same characteristics your Inner Child has now. The dreams you had and the adventures you wanted are those of your Inner Child.

What your chronological age is right now doesn't matter; you still have a sweet, innocent, loving Inner Child within you making a ruckus about something it wants. Even as an adult, if nurtured properly, your Inner Child will enjoy many of the typical traits associated with a normal, well-adjusted child.

Your Inner Child is a separate voice within your mind, just as your physical body separates you from your physical parents.

This distinction is very important to understand when Self-Parenting. Due to the subtle nature of your Inner Conversations the Inner Parent often forgets that its Inner Child voice is as separate and distinct as a real child would be.

The half-hour Self-Parenting sessions will teach you how to distinguish between the two Inner Voices. As you begin to work more consciously with your Inner Conversations you will recognize the autonomy of your Inner Child. It is easy to forget this important fact in the beginning, but your understanding will grow with practice.

The Positive Inner Child

One of the greatest strengths of the Inner Child is ENTHUSIASM! Don't you see every young child you know running here and there, never stopping; climbing everything, picking up anything, and constantly pushing buttons on phones, televisions, and videos?

Children are curious and enthusiastic about everything (except slowing down) and are constantly seeking to discover and explore new territories.

This trait is VERY IMPORTANT because it is this enthusiasm, or excitement, which gives both your Selves the energetic feelings of well-being and happiness that are essential qualities of living life.

The Inner Parent may be able to experience moderate levels of satisfaction by itself, but the Inner Child controls the true emotional energy of enthusiasm or bliss. Many of you enjoyed these feelings as children, but as adults have learned to deny them for practical reasons or simply have forgotten how to enjoy positive feelings because of your negative Self-Parenting.

Your Inner Child loves to have fun and in this way it desires activities similar to those of an outer child. Your Inner Child will find joy and fulfillment in the simplest pleasures. It loves playing games and play-acting.

Learning and practicing new skills such as coloring, drawing, and painting are all pleasurable activities enjoyed by your Inner Child. He or she loves to explore new environments such as the beauty and treasures found in nature.

The positive Inner Child is anxious to learn and only needs to be taught and shown.

Another wonderful quality or trait of your Inner Child is its natural affection and willingness to please. When the outer parent demonstrates affection and acknowledgment of the outer child, he or she is usually willing to do just about anything the parent wants. In this same way your Inner Child also has a deep desire to please you (the Inner Parent). Under ideal conditions it will be willing to do or learn just about anything your Inner Parent asks.

The Inner Child has other important strengths or traits equally as valuable for the Inner Parent to understand when Self-Parenting. However, they **ARE NOT** related to normal aspects of outer childhood. These are better understood as traits that are unique and special to the Inner Child voice alone.

The Inner Child is in charge of and controls the emotions and the energies for the two Selves.

Your emotional feelings best reveal the voice of the Inner Child within you. The variety and scope of your emotions, ranging between love/hate through excitement/boredom, are the exclusive province of the Inner Child. Your Inner Child is the vital source of enthusiasm for both Selves. However, this understanding might not sit too easily with an Inner Parent who is used to thinking it can dominate or control the emotions of the Inner Child through logic or will power.

It is very important for the Inner Parent to understand that the Inner Child is the owner of the feelings. You (the Inner Parent) cannot experience an emotion unless it is given or fed to you by the Inner Child in your Inner Conversations. All the emotions that come from "you" are actually coming from your Inner Child. The Inner Parent may act on the information provided by the emotions but it is your Inner Child that originally feels them.

The Inner Child is also the voice and simplistic logic of that part of us most in touch with the physical body. It has been described as the animal self of man. This Self adds to your overall personality through its experiences of the five senses. It records all the raw data received by the five senses into the subconscious mind. Incredible amounts of information about your past can be remembered by your Inner Child since it already has these memories stored in its data banks.

If you enjoyed a high degree of nurturing and support as you grew into adulthood, your own Inner Child will retain much of its original enthusiasm for living. As an adult, you will continue to experience life with a freshness and joy that only the eyes of a child can see.

The Negative Inner Child

The outer child that has been neglected, beaten, abused physically or mentally, and has experienced other forms of negative emotional programming has received a poor start in life. Its "eager to please" attitude disappears and is replaced by resistant and rebellious behavior seemingly in complete opposition to anything the parent desires. In the same way, if you as an Inner Parent are mean, abusive, or demanding when Self-Parenting your Inner Child, it will bring the negative behaviors of resistance and rebellion into your Inner Conversations.

The Inner Child will then be unwilling to learn or to listen to the wants and desires of you, the Inner Parent.

If your Inner Child is being suppressed by your Inner Parent this will put a damper on the amount of enthusiasm and energy available to you. Denial of the spontaneous emotions or feelings of your Inner Child causes the energy and enthusiasm needed by both Selves to disappear.

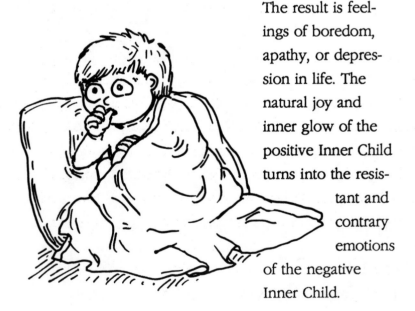

The result is feelings of boredom, apathy, or depression in life. The natural joy and inner glow of the positive Inner Child turns into the resistant and contrary emotions of the negative Inner Child.

The Inner Child tends to make simplistic
decisions and interpretations about life based on its
experiences with the five senses (for example, whether
it feels good or not).

It is not as experienced as the Inner Parent and,
just like an outer child, it does not have the education,
training, or capability to reason with the understanding
and wisdom of an adult. Because the Inner Child lacks
experience and intellectual maturity it depends on feelings and emotions when it comes to decision making.

Since it relies solely on emotions, your Inner
Child can harbor irrational ideas or programming in its
memory banks. These are usually the result of a severe
trauma, such as an accident, separation, or death of a
loved one, which emotionally overloads the senses.
With its limited reasoning abilities the Inner Child can't
make sense of such an intense trauma. Consequently, it
stores the emotional "charge" of the trauma with a
simplistic explanation, when a more abstract parental
interpretation may be required.

Unfortunately, these irrational ideas continue to influence the Inner Child's future thinking and decision making within your Inner Conversations. They prevent the Inner Child's natural energies of affection and playfulness from flowing smoothly and enthusiastically. Psychologists have long recognized these negative emotional traumas in outer children and associated these experiences and their aftereffects with different problems.

Even if the Inner Parent is neutral concerning the effects of the event, the trauma may still exist within the Inner Child. To be healed successfully it must be resolved within the Inner Conversations, and can be through the conscious rationalization of positive Self-Parenting.

Left unchecked and free to influence your Inner Conversations, the negative Inner Child can turn an otherwise normal person into a compulsive spender, or an alcoholic. It can cause any variety of addictive impulsive behaviors such as food binging, excessive dieting, or chemical dependencies.

When this happens the energies of the negative Inner Child completely dominate your Inner Conversations to the detriment of both Selves.

As a person gets older, the voice of his or her Inner Child may also simply fade from oversight or inattention. It is not desirable for this condition to become permanent however, for such a person will not be able to experience joy and happiness in life.

It is possible for anyone to get back in touch with their negative Inner Child if their Inner Parent will begin a program of Self-Parenting Exercises. These half-hour sessions are designed to reintroduce you to your Inner Child and provide methods for removing the reasons why your Inner Child became negative in the first place.

The Ideal Role of the Inner Child

The Inner Child does not have an ideal role. It only needs to be itself. Yet in many cases the voice of the Inner Child has been suppressed, ridiculed, or punished so often that it has psychologically retreated to safety. Or the Inner Parent has silenced the Inner Child in the name of being "grown up."

As a result it can sometimes be difficult for a suppressed Inner Child to once again feel safe enough to start expressing and exposing its feelings after suffering this kind of chronic abuse.

Do you recall receiving any parenting that made you negative as a child? Were you forced to go to bed too early, made to eat food you didn't like, not allowed to go to the movies with your friends, or punished for things you didn't do? Were you ignored, neglected, physically or mentally abused, or prevented from expressing or fulfilling an important need?

If you were to experience the same quality of parenting from your outer parents today, you would feel as negative about it now as you did then.

Yet many of you continue this same style of Self-Parenting within your Inner Conversations.

In order for healing to begin, your Inner Child's negative feelings concerning these or other experiences must be recognized, accepted, and understood by the Inner Parent. Negative feelings from your Inner Child are simply the result of poor conditioning or programming. Negative emotional reactions are symptoms or indicators of destructive Self-Parenting patterns that, once corrected, will result in increased happiness and contentment for the Inner Child.

To correct problems of this nature the Inner Child must be made to feel safe again. The responsibility to change a negative Inner Child lies directly with the Inner Parent. Devoting a half-hour a day to the Self-Parenting Exercises gives the Inner Parent time to love and nurture the Inner Child so that its voice can once again be heard without negative judgments.

The key to positive Self-Parenting in your Inner Conversations is for you, as the Inner Parent, to take the initiative and become a receiver for the voice of the Inner Child. This is the first step of developing an intimate awareness of your Inner Child and its role in your Self-Parenting.

Practical steps for this process will be outlined as the book progresses and powerful techniques and methods to achieve this purpose will be described in Part III.

Without the knowledge
and rational thinking processes
of the Inner Parent, the Inner
Child has only a limited ability to
reason. Without the Inner Child
the Inner Parent is left without
emotional response or
capability.

If you don't have as
much energy and enthusiasm for
living as you did when you were
a child, it's time to reawaken that
little person inside you.

Practice the Self-Parenting Exercises in
Part III and you will consistently enjoy your daily life
and all it has to offer. Working together, the nurturing
Inner Parent and the enthusiastic Inner Child can
become powerful allies.

LISTENING
TO YOUR
INNER
CONVERSATIONS

4

You are now becoming familiar with the
two participants of your Inner Conversations: the
Inner Parent and the Inner Child.

In this chapter you will "take a listen" to some
deeper and more powerful examples of Inner Conversations in which both the Inner Parent and the Inner
Child display some examples of their respective traits
and personalities.

It will be invaluable for you to begin listening to
deeper levels of the internal dialogue occurring
between you, as the Inner Parent, and you, as the
Inner Child.

You must explore the deeper levels

of your Inner Conversations to achieve self-understanding. The Self-Parenting Exercises in Part III will help you un-cover the deeper feelings and more fundamental attitudes of your Inner Parent. The initial benefit will be increased self-knowledge, a prerequisite for your happiness and success in life. But more than that, be-coming more aware of your Inner Conversations is an indispensable tool for resolving Inner Conflicts that are hurting you by limiting your life.

If you want security, peace of mind, and personal happiness, positive Self-Parenting in your Inner Conversations will provide the foundation.

Once aware of your Inner Conversations and its participants, you will start noticing more occasions when both Selves are conversing. Many of your Inner Conversations during the day will be simple and ordinary: deciding what to wear in the morning, what to have for breakfast, whether or not to read the paper before work. Routine Inner Conversations are very subtle but you will start hearing them when you (the Inner Parent) begin paying attention to them.

The Inner Parent and Inner Child also have arguments, known as Inner Conflicts.

With their different personalities and desires, the two Selves will many times desire opposite outcomes for the same set of circumstances. They can easily disagree or be in conflict with each other. It is most important to be aware of and acknowledge Inner Conflicts when they are happening inside your mind.

Your two Inner Selves (each with their separate and distinct needs) make up the person you think you are. In order to begin true Self-Parenting, you must actually get to know two separate Selves and how each responds to the other as they interact within your Inner Conversations.

One easy way to tune into your Inner Conversations is to become aware of how frequently they occur in response to circumstances in the outside world. You often acknowledge and describe your Inner Conflicts when talking to others, even though you may not have been aware of all their complexities. Before learning about your Inner Conversations you might have experienced this phenomenon of conflict between the two Selves.

For example, how often have you or someone you know said:

"Part of me wants to _____ , and part of me wants to_____ ."

Translated this means:

"My Inner Parent wants to

_____ ,

and my Inner Child wants to

_____ ."

Or what about this
saying:

**"The spirit is willing but the
flesh is weak."**

This statement really
means,

"My Inner Parent thinks it's a great
idea, but my Inner Child does not
want to provide the energy."

Many colloquial expressions indicate two
different sets of desires or needs inside your mind.

One of the more famous from affairs of the heart is:

> **"I love you but I'm not 'in love' with you."**

Your Inner Conversation is actually saying:

> "My Inner Parent thinks you are a great guy (or girl) and likes you tremendously as a person, but my Inner Child just can't get enthusiastic or excited enough about being with you sexually."

Many other examples of Inner Conversations can be found in the media. In the comics section of the Sunday papers you will often see the two Inner Selves being expressed, especially in the comics "Feiffer" and "Cathy." Many songs on the top-ten charts are faithful reproductions of strong and emotional Inner Conversations set to music. Classic movies and plays always feature characters that personify, in an outer way, the Inner Parent and Inner Child voices within us all. Films by Woody Allen contain many examples of dialogue representing Inner Conversations. As you make progress with the Self-Parenting Exercises you will see and hear frequent examples of Inner Conversations being reflected in the outer world.

The differences between your Inner Parent and your Inner Child are really quite simple to discern.

During the activities of your day notice how and when you make decisions in your mind using your Inner Conversations as a guide. Your Inner Parent will provide rational discussions and reasoning that sound just like the kinds your parents would have used. When your Inner Parent becomes upset he or she may order, warn, lecture, analyze, blame, or otherwise Self-Parent your Inner Child with the same parental perspectives you received as a child.

Your Inner Child is the voice of "I want." This voice in your mind acts and reacts spontaneously and emotionally. Your Inner Child "wants what it wants when it wants it." All of a sudden it will want a candy bar, think of a television show, or stop to admire clothes in a store window when you (the Inner Parent) are in a hurry.

If its needs are not being met it will demand constant attention or complain of being hungry, thirsty, cold, or bored. Its reactions and demands inside your mind will duplicate those you made many times as an outer child.

There are formal and informal ways to begin listening to your Inner Conversations.

The easiest method is simply to take some paper and start writing them down. Take a few minutes, look out the window, and write down what one side of your mind says on the left side of the paper, and what the other side says on the right. Write down whatever dialogue you hear in your mind just as you hear it. Since your Inner Conversations are going on all the time anyway, it's effortless to record what they say. Don't be concerned with which voice is saying what, just write it down.

After you have written a page or two, go back and analyze which voice was which. The separation between your Inner Parent and your Inner Child will be quite distinct. You will be able to see the familiar patterns of the two personalities asserting themselves within you.

As you become more familiar with your Inner Parent and Inner Child you can practice writing down Inner Conversations on an **Inner Conversation Dialogue Sheet**. This is an ordinary piece of paper with the following headings at the top and a vertical line down the middle:

INNER CONVERSATION DIALOGUE SHEET

Date	Subject
Inner Parent	**Inner Child**

Inner Parent	Inner Child
Needs of the Inner Parent	**Needs of the Inner Child**

You will find the Inner Conversation Dialogue Sheet a very effective way to differentiate between the two voices. When you become more confident about which voice is which, put your typical "parental" sounding comments under the Inner Parent column. Put your typical "child" sounding comments under the Inner Child. Once you have practiced writing out your Inner Conversations a few times, it becomes easier to mentally follow both sides when you are performing activities in your daily life.

The **Inner Conversation** on the next page was written down by a Self-Parenting student while waiting a few minutes for a bus.

Inner Parent	Inner Child
●	Look at that person in the wheel chair.
Yeah, that's too bad.	
	Look at their thin legs.
Just be glad you don't have that problem.	
	Believe me I am.
We've got to get downtown or we'll ● be late for our appointment.	
	We're not going to get there on time anyway. Besides that guy is never on time.
I know but it's still bad to be late for appointments.	
●	A cab will get us there on time. It would be more fun too.
Nah, too expensive.	
	Look at that!

How many thousands of Inner Conversations have you had just like that one?

Although it may not be of major significance, it is a typical example of many Inner Conversations you might have during the day in just a few seconds. As you become more involved in Self-Parenting you will hear much mundane talk. Other Inner Conversations will have more action and intensity, such as the following example.

The next **Inner Conversation** illustrates the ramification of an Inner Conflict inside your mind. Until now, most of the Inner Conversations have been light and easy.

OTHER *INNER CONVERSATIONS* WILL HAVE MORE ACTION AND INTENSITY SUCH AS THE FOLLOWING *INNER CONVERSATION* RECORDED BY A STUDENT WHOSE INNER CHILD WANTED TO GO SKIING BUT WHOSE INNER PARENT KNEW SHE WAS SUPPOSED TO BE STUDYING FOR A TEST.

A FEMALE STUDENT'S *INNER CONVERSATION* DURING THE DAY...

WHAT ARE YOU GOING TO DO ABOUT THE TEST NEXT WEEK?

WHAT ARE YOU TALKING ABOUT?

YOU KNOW. HOW CAN WE GO SKIING IF WE HAVE A TEST?

WHO CARES ABOUT A STUPID TEST. I HAVE A CHANCE TO GO SKIING WITH BILL AND GET TO KNOW HIM BETTER.

When first listening to your Inner
Conversations, it is very important for you to hear and
accept **both** sides of your Inner Conversations, even if
one Inner Voice is expressing a negative opinion or
weakness.

If you, as the Inner Parent, try to negate or
ignore the negative voice of your Inner Child, you will
be unable to successfully Self-Parent. When the Inner
Parent does not listen to the Inner Child, it will have
the same types of problems that an outer parent has
who doesn't really listen to his or her child.

HOW ABOUT THIS *INNER CONVERSATION* WHICH A SELF-PARENTING STUDENT RECORDED AT A "SWINGING SINGLES" NIGHT SPOT.

A SINGLE MALE'S *INNER CONVERSATION...*

T he next **Inner Conversation** was submitted by a newspaper reporter working late to meet a deadline. His Inner Parent knows he needs the money for survival, yet at the same time his Inner Child hates the job.

Inner Parent	Inner Child
	I'm bored and I HATE THIS JOB!
I know, I know, believe me I know. But we have more work to do.	
	I don't care.
You will when we don't have enough money to buy food or pay the rent.	
	Let's finish this later.
I can't. We have a deadline to meet.	
	Nobody is going to read this.
The editor will. He complained last week about a piece we did. Pretty heavily if you will remember.	
	Yeah, yeah... He's a jerk anyway. What does he know about life. He is a workaholic boozer

	as it is.
Right. (still working)	
	I thought we were going to quit this dead end, low life, go nowhere job.
Right. Who's going to pay the rent then. Mother Goose or Father Gander?	
	We have money saved.
Oh yeah, We can last at least 30 days on what we've got saved, maybe 31.	

Many of your Inner Conversations are not happily resolved because your Self-Parenting is negative and non-nurturing to your Inner Child. The less nurturing your Inner Parent is throughout the day, the more difficulty you will have feeling personal happiness in your life.

The following **Inner Conversation** was written by a student one quiet night. It demonstrates how unthoughtful, uncaring, and unaware Self-Parenting in an Inner Conversation can be. Sadly, many of us (Inner Parents) do this to ourselves (Inner Children) on a regular basis.

Inner Parent	Inner Child
●	I feel sad.
Why?	
	I don't know. I just do.
Don't be ridiculous. There is nothing for you to feel sad about.	
	I just feel like crying.
I can't believe how stupid you are.	
	(silence)
● You are being stupid. What do you feel sad about?	
	Nothing, it doesn't matter.
●	

When Self-Parenting in
your Inner Conversa-
tions, always remember
that the Inner Child
voice represents your
feelings.

If you are feeling emotionally sad,
hurt, angry, or upset, it is really
the Inner Child that is feeling this
way.

If you, as an Inner Parent, are not considerate of
the feelings of your Inner Child, after awhile your
Inner Child will become numb to its feelings. At this
point if you ask how it is feeling it may simply reply,
"Fine," in a dull monotone. There will be no other
emotional response that it feels safe in making. If it
becomes chronic, this negative Self-Parenting within
your Inner Conversations will create a depressed or
suppressed personality.

Many times an Inner Parent has an "I-told-you-so" attitude about the feelings of the Inner Child.

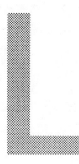ook at what happens in this **Inner Conversation** of a seventeen-year-old student hoping a new love interest will call:

Inner Parent	Inner Child
	Why hasn't Peter rung?
I told you he wouldn't	
	But he said he liked me.
And you believed him?	
	Sort of.
You know they are all the same. Why do you continue with all this false hope?	
	He's different.
Oh, good one!	
	I'm feeling lonely.
You should ring him and see what he's doing.	
	Oh no, that's okay.
So then, what do you want to do?	
	I don't know.
Forget him. He's like all the rest.	
	I love him!
Oh god, not again.	

In this example of Self-Parenting it is clear that this person's Inner Parent is not nurturing her Inner Child by allowing it to express its feelings. Without the support of its Inner Parent, many times an Inner Child will be too afraid to express itself further.

Notice how the previous Inner Conversations are typical examples of the thoughts you might have had in similar situations. Your Inner Conversations may or may not be typical, but one thing is for sure, they will be your own and they will be going on deep inside your mind.

You will become increasingly in tune with your Inner Conversations as you take time during your day to listen to them. When you start having private sessions with your Inner Child and practicing the Self-Parenting Exercises in Part III, your progress listening to and understanding your Inner Conversations will be rapid.

As your awareness increases, you will be able to graduate to the second stage of Self-Parenting in your Inner Conversations. You will have enough experience to learn how to balance your Inner Conversations during times of the dreaded **INNER CONFLICT**.

PART II
INNER CONFLICTS

5

INNER CONFLICTS: PROBLEMS WITH YOUR INNER CONVERSATIONS

Most of us have at least a few problems in our lives.

Outer problems such as paying the rent, overdue bills, finding a suitable job, or ending a relationship can set you back temporarily. Even though these outer problems are traumatic and can cause stress, you recognize what is wrong and are able to mobilize your energy to handle the situations. Since outer problems are "out there" you can direct the considerable energies of your body and mind to solving them.

Inner Conflicts, on the other hand, can be devastating. Since they are "in" your mind, they confuse your ability to think clearly. Inner Conflicts create indecision and cause a physical and mental paralysis that can overwhelm your ability to produce or perform as a human being. The issues of an Inner Conflict can last a lifetime if they are not recognized and handled properly.

Inner Conflicts cannot be settled by changing events or circumstances outside your mind. An Inner Conflict over lack of money (such as needing money to build self-esteem or to please others) will not be solved by getting more money. Although more money might solve an outer conflict, having a million dollars in the bank won't solve an Inner Conflict over money. One half of your Inner Conversation will only want two million.

Trying to solve any type of an Inner Conflict with an outer solution will only bring the same unsuccessful results.

The worst part about Inner Conflicts is that they are self-inflicted. You are doing the damage to yourself, all by yourself, within your Inner Conversations. Until you do the work to pull yourself out, you will remain stuck with an Inner Conflict despite the help and best intentions of your family, friends, or even professional intervention.

The good news is that you can now resolve your Inner Conflicts by following the steps in this book and practicing the Self-Parenting Exercises in Part III.

Inner Conflicts are created as a result of a clash between the needs of your Inner Parent and the needs of your Inner Child.

If the conflicting needs between the two Selves are strong enough, you will experience an Inner Conflict as the major problem in your life. Any chronic, persistent, or negative Inner Conversation is a result of this conflict. Physical, emotional, mental, or social paralysis always accompanies Inner Conflict.

Since they are two different personalities, many times the Inner Parent and Inner Child have conflicting needs. The Inner Child wants chocolate ice cream because it tastes good and the Inner Parent wants to eat vanilla yogurt for health reasons. Or, the Inner Child wants to sleep in because it's tired and the Inner Parent says to go to work so it won't get fired. The Inner Child wants to buy new clothes to look good but the Inner Parent wants to spend the money on new tires for the car. The Inner Parent wants to go to school in Chicago but the Inner Child wants to live near the beach.

With the increasing complexity of modern life, different and unusual types of Inner Conflicts are emerging. For example, a female Inner Parent may want to get married because her biological clock is running out, but her Inner Child doesn't like the only logical marriage choice. Or, an Inner Parent wants to further her career by taking a job promotion, but this will disrupt the desires of the Inner Child to start a family. In another twist, the Inner Parent (female) may want to have a family but the **Inner Child** wants to further **its** career.

Your situation will depend on the unique styles and issues of the participants in *your* Self-Parenting.

During an Inner Conflict, neither side has a clear-cut advantage; the two voices are stalemated. Ideally the physical and emotional manifestations of the Inner Conflict will alert the Inner Parent to investigate the Inner Conversation by writing it down.

If you are emotionally or mentally immobilized, frantic, unable to make a decision, definitely not sure, or generally unable to choose a clearly defined path regarding a situation, you are experiencing the dreaded Inner Conflict.

Inner Conflicts usually involve a situation where your Inner Selves are scared or have to make a decision, but they are paralyzed as to what move to make next. This often results in feelings of guilt or obligation. As a result, your Inner Parent and Inner Child experience a conflicting set of needs hanging both of them up. For one reason or another, each Self prevents the other Self from realizing its needs.

The two Selves get into such a mental stew over the problem that neither of them can win over the other, so both end up losing.

Inner Conflicts must be resolved. There is no getting around it. Both sides are together in the relationship and both Inner Selves have needs that must be met! Until both Selves are satisfied, neither the Inner Parent nor the Inner Child will be able to function effectively. If one Inner Self wins over the needs of the other, there will be a backlash from the other Inner Self which will be harmful and damaging to the Self-Parenting relationship.

A simple, powerful, and overlooked message in modern society is that needs form the basis of living. If you have a need you will be temporarily unhappy until it is fulfilled. If you have a primary need that is not fulfilled, you will remain unhappy even if all your other needs are successfully met. On a subtler level, if your Inner Parent or Inner Child has an important need, it must be met. Or that Self (in the Inner Conversation) will never be happy—no matter what else happens.

Special awareness and techniques must be applied during Inner Conflicts. These Self-Parenting techniques involve problem-solving methods developed by psychologists to resolve outer conflicts; however, as an Inner Parent, you will learn to focus these methods inwardly to resolve your conflict of needs.

First of all, whenever you realize you are locked into an emotional/mental Inner Conflict do the following:

STOP,
LISTEN,
and WRITE DOWN
YOUR INNER
CONVERSATION.

This step must be taken by your Inner Parent. It is your Inner Parent's responsibility to assess the intensity of your Inner Conflict.

If the Inner Conflict is of sufficient magnitude, your Inner Parent

MUST
MAKE an
INNER
CONVERSATION
DIALOGUE SHEET.

This allows the two Selves to sit down and write out the Inner Conflict that is inevitably going on in your mind (and in your body, too, by this time).

Four outcomes are possible for resolving an Inner Conflict. Many of you may already be familiar with the four conflict resolution options as used in outer problem solving. The Self-Parenting workshops have developed a specialized process to use these options for resolving the conflict of needs between the Inner Parent and Inner Child. The four possible outcomes are:

1. Lose/Lose

In the Lose/Lose solution neither your Inner Parent nor your Inner Child has their needs met. The Inner Conflict is not resolved to the satisfaction of either Self.

2. Win/Lose

In this situation your Inner Parent wins and your Inner Child loses. Your Inner Parent uses its position of power to make sure its needs are met even at the expense of the Inner Child.

3. Lose/Win

Using this solution, your Inner Parent loses and your Inner Child wins. The needs of your Inner Parent are not met but your Inner Child gets exactly what it wants.

4. Win/Win

In this case the needs of both your Inner Parent and your Inner Child are met. Whatever needs were in conflict, thus creating the crisis in the first place, are resolved to the satisfaction of both Selves.

The ideal Self-Parenting resolution for all your Inner Conflicts is the Win/Win solution. If you are a strong person with an intimate understanding of your Inner Conversations, you can always resolve Inner Conflicts with a Win/Win solution.

6

RESOLVING INNER CONFLICTS: ONE MAN'S STORY

This chapter chronicles the experience of an advanced Self-Parenting student confronted with a "real life" Inner Conflict.

A real estate agent began to develop a major Inner Conflict resulting from the needs of his Inner Parent involving his job and the requirements of his Inner Child for some leisure time.

Here is what happened.

A weekend real estate seminar in the city was approaching and there had been a recent snowstorm in a popular ski area. This person's Inner Parent had been planning ahead for his future and intended to go the seminar; it would be the only one for the next six months. His Inner Parent knew that this weekend would inspire and improve his performance (and income) at work.

His Inner Child, on the other hand, had developed an intense desire to go skiing. It hadn't been skiing yet this season and went only once last year. His Inner Child realized that due to other scheduling this upcoming weekend would be its last chance to ski for the next two months.

It had had enough of work Monday through Friday and was demanding some fun for a change. It also did not relish the prospect of working the next twelve days in a row, much less not going skiing. And for this Inner Child the seminar definitely equated to work.

The result was the following **Inner Conflict,** as demonstrated by the points of view the Self-Parenting student recorded on his Inner Conversation Dialogue Sheet.

Four potential solutions could be worked out from this "real life" situation which would reflect the four possibilities of Inner Conflict resolution. In your experience with similar situations you also resolved your Inner Conflicts with one of the following solutions:

LOSE/LOSE

Unfortunately, Lose/Lose is the option that a lot of us unconsciously use to resolve our Inner Conflicts. Lose/lose is more a process of passively doing nothing until pressures implode than an active process of conflict resolution. In this solution neither the Inner Parent nor the Inner Child have their needs met.

The Lose/Lose situation usually involves sabotage by one of the Inner Selves that ruins it for both. In the Inner Conflict above the following Self-Parenting could easily have taken place:

The real estate saleman's Inner Parent simply decides unilaterally that he is going to attend the seminar and completely ignores the pleas, feelings, and needs of his Inner Child. The Inner Parent is determined to go, but his needs are being met at the expense of his Inner Child.

Remember, however, that the Inner Child controls the energy levels and bodily processes. On Wednesday night it starts building up resistance and stress in the body with the goal of not attending the seminar. By Friday evening the real estate agent is so congested and weak from lack of energy that he is too sick to attend the seminar. As a result his Inner Parent reluctantly gives in and cancels his plans.

In this Self-Parenting resolution both parties lose. The Inner Parent (as well as the Inner Child) misses out on an important seminar that is crucial to his future, and the Inner Child (as well as the Inner Parent) doesn't get to go skiing. Neither Self has any of its needs met.

WIN/LOSE

Win/Lose Self-Parenting is a victory for the Inner Parent but a loss for the needs of the Inner Child. In the above situation the agent's Inner Parent continues to intend signing up for the seminar against the wishes and needs of the Inner Child. When the Inner Child starts to manifest its physical symptoms of resistance and rebellion the Inner Parent simply pushes through those symptoms using will power and determination.

In order to push through and "win" over his Inner Child the Inner Parent might read a book on colds and force-feed himself thousands of milligrams of Vitamin C. He could initiate a complete food fast to cleanse himself of the toxins created by his Inner Child.

If he was a strong Inner Parent he might even wind up forcing both Selves to attend the seminar while sick. Somehow, someway, the Inner Parent would use will power to dominate the situation and make sure he attended the seminar, dragging his Inner Child along for the ride.

LOSE/WIN

Lose/Win Self-Parenting is a loss for the needs of the person's Inner Parent but a victory for the needs of his Inner Child.

In this situation the Inner Child has many ways of getting his needs met. He might hold up his end of the Inner Conflict too well. After the unilateral Self-Parenting decision by the Inner Parent to attend the seminar, the Inner Child could start nagging with an undercurrent of whining that would soon become a loud roar. By Wednesday the Inner Child could create so many physical symptoms and problems, a weak Inner Parent would cancel the seminar.

On Friday after a missed deadline, an extraordinary and miraculous recovery would occur just in time to be on the slopes early Saturday morning. Even if the Inner Child couldn't ultimately go skiing he might at least have time for some fun or social needs to be met. He could go out on a date or see a movie he wouldn't have had time for otherwise.

Thus the person's Inner Child is happy because his needs are met, but the needs of his Inner Parent go unfulfilled.

WIN/WIN

The ideal Self-Parenting resolution is the Win/Win option in which the needs of both the Inner Parent and the Inner Child are met. This occurs when each Inner Voice of the Inner Conversation gets exactly what it needs and wants. Win/Win could also occur as the result of a compromise through which both Inner Voices accept an alternate solution.

Although option four is the most satisfying choice, it takes a skilled and committed Inner Parent to pull it off. The two Selves must communicate their needs to each other, and agree that each set of needs has the right to be fulfilled.

How This Inner Conflict Was Resolved

In this case the Self-Parenting student recognized that he was suffering from an Inner Conflict. As the Inner Parent he had decided unilaterally to go to the seminar. As his Inner Child began to manifest symptoms of resistance by getting sick he noticed the two Selves arguing back and forth inside his mind and realized something was wrong.

He took the time to write "Inner Conversation Dialogue Sheet" on the top of a piece of paper and

started

writing out

his Inner

Conversation.

Since he had also been doing his half-hour of private Self-Parenting sessions each day and was acutely sensitive to the needs and desires of his Inner Child, he recognized the characteristic rebellion and resistance that he knew to be typical of his Inner Child.

Feeling and reading the signals his Inner Child was sending through the way his body felt, he wrote them down on the Inner Conversation Dialogue Sheet. Thus, he became aware of his Inner Conflict as well as the needs of both his Inner Parent and Inner Child. As a result of writing out his Inner Conversation the following facts became obvious:

One: His Inner Parent didn't care about missing work, it just didn't want to miss the seminar.

Two: His Inner Child was happy enough to go to the seminar but it didn't want to spend all its time working and not having fun. Plus, the Inner Child's need to go skiing was too powerful to ignore.

Three: The Inner Selves agreed that it was somehow possible for both of them to have their needs met.

The Self-Parenting student then guided his two Inner Selves through a problem-solving session making sure that each Self was getting full expression of needs. Once awareness had surfaced through the Inner Conversation Dialogue Sheet, the following Self-Parenting solution took form.

Final Result of the Win/Win Solution

The real estate agent decided to take two days off work and go skiing on Thursday and Friday. Both Selves then agreed to happily attend the seminar on Saturday and Sunday.

In this situation each Inner Self was happy, maybe even ecstatic. The Inner Parent went to the seminar which he knew was important and shouldn't be missed. He also went skiing, took two days off, and was quite happy not to be working twelve days in a row.

His Inner Child on the other hand not only got to go skiing, but left two days earlier to ski in fresher snow, with much less crowded weekday conditions.

You won't see this Inner Child getting sick on Wednesday. No way! With this Win/Win solution both Selves win, neither side loses, and the needs of both Selves are fully met. Positive Self-Parenting was the key to resolving this Inner Conflict.

Although this solution may now seem simple or obvious, it is worthwhile to note that if this was your own Inner Conflict with your unique circumstances it would not be so easy to flesh out a Win/Win solution. Part of the problem with an Inner Conflict seems to be that the person having it is the most blind to working out a solution.

Many beginning and intermediate Self-Parenting students fully understand the intellectual dynamics of an Inner Conflict, and yet when they are having one, they are too preoccupied by it to recognize the symptoms. The above resolution demonstrates very sophisticated awareness, understanding, and skill in resolving Inner Conflicts which you can acquire as well.

7

EIGHT STEPS
OF INNER
CONFLICT
RESOLUTION

The key to resolving Inner Conflicts is positive Self-Parenting for the needs of both Inner Selves.

Your Inner Parent must take responsibility for solving Inner Conflicts that arise. Your Inner Child can't do it because it doesn't know how. People in the outside world can't do it because they can't hear the Inner Conflict inside your mind. Besides, they don't know you as well as you know yourself.

Your Inner Parent is the Inner Self with the strongest motivation to:

One: Recognize an Inner Conflict.

Two: Use Win/Win Self-Parenting methods to resolve the conflict successfully.

However, in the typical Inner Conflict the unaware or untrained Inner Parent unknowingly uses the Win/Lose method to resolve conflicts. This may temporarily satisfy the short-term needs of the Inner Parent, but of course, it is bad for the long-term needs of the Inner Child.

Occasionally a strong Inner Child will create a Lose/Lose or Lose/Win situation to salvage its self-respect. But these three Self-Parenting methods are unsatisfactory for the optimum functioning of both Selves. Within your Inner Conversations, either Self making a conflict resolution decision on its own invites failure.

The Inner Parent has the major responsibility for Self-Parenting in Inner Conflicts.

Its role is to make decisions, choose options, and evaluate the important aspects of your life. For best results however, it must do this with the cooperative input and energies of the Inner Child. If your Inner Parent tries to Self-Parent without the cooperation of your Inner Child, it will fail. You, as the Inner Parent, must assume the role of loving, supporting, and nurturing your Inner Child.

By doing so you can make your life full and satisfying for the first time since you were a child and keep it that way for the rest of your life.

Any time you have a severe Inner Conflict you will need to take the following Self-Parenting steps, in sequence, to establish and fulfill the needs of both your Inner Parent and your Inner Child. Similar problem-solving methods have long been established by psychologists and negotiators for use in resolving the conflicts in outer relationships. These methods are adapted here for resolving Inner Conflicts in your Inner Conversations through positive Self-Parenting.

Step One:

Recognition by your Inner Parent that you have an Inner Conflict.

Your Inner Parent realizes you are trapped in an Inner Conflict when your body, emotions, and mind are immobilized by inactivity, indecision, or a constant, heated Inner Conversation that remains unresolved.

Your mind may be involved in an Inner Conflict for hours, days, or weeks. But until your Inner Parent consciously recognizes this fact and takes steps to correct it, your Inner Parent and Inner Child will continue to mentally do battle.

Step Two:
Your Inner Parent makes the decision to postively Self-Parent your Inner Conflict by writing out your Inner Conversation.

Your Inner Conflict involves a conflict of needs between your two Selves, but sometimes it is difficult to determine what those needs are unless the Inner Conversation is written out in an objective manner.

This is why the **Inner Conversation Dialogue Sheet** was created. Writing down the Inner Conflict on paper—in your own handwriting—clarifies the demands and arguments of the two Selves. Step Two makes it easier for you to objectively determine what needs underlie the arguments of the two Selves and will help you determine how you are blocking your creativity or productivity. Enough time must be taken during Step Two to write down your entire Inner Conversation carefully and completely.

Step Three:
List the specific needs of each Inner Self.

Once the comments (and complaints!) of each Self are written down, you can determine what the specific needs of each Self are on the back of your **Inner Conversation Dialogue Sheet**.

Both sides must have their needs met. This Self-Parenting is crucial for returning your Inner Conversation to its normal, happy, and productive state. Many times your Inner Parent will be unwilling to give in to the demands of the Inner Child because they seem so outrageous. But underlying the demands are real needs, and once you discover the true needs of your Inner Child you will naturally want to fulfill them.

The primary needs of your Inner Child are for physical or emotional comfort, security, stimulation, physical contact, love, attention, approval, or acceptance. One or more of these basic needs will always underlie even the most outrageous demands or wants of your Inner Child.

Step Four:

Your Inner Parent and Inner Child mutually decide and agree that the solution for this Inner Conflict must be acceptable to both Selves.

Once the needs are clear, the two Selves must agree to help and support each other to satisfy those needs. Sometimes this is the hardest step when it could be the easiest, because the Inner Parent or Inner Child will not give up its desire to win at any cost.

Special care, practice, and consideration must be taken to establish this cooperation between the two Selves before going on to Step Five.

Step Five:

The Inner Selves search together for solutions to the Inner Conflict.

Positive Self-Parenting will focus on ways of meeting the needs of both Selves. Generate as many ideas as possible to accomplish and accommodate the needs of each Self during this step.

The key to Step Five is to be creative. List in two columns as many solutions as possible which meet the needs of your Inner Parent and your Inner Child. During this step list any solutions that meet the needs of either Self, even if they are impractical or don't help the other Self. Generating as many solutions as possible stirs the creative juices of both Selves to solve their mutual problems.

Sometimes you may simply need more information to solve your Inner Conflict. You will need to talk to friends, ask advice from experts, read books, do research, or make phone calls. Be willing to do whatever it takes to find answers and potential solutions for the needs of both Selves.

Step Six:
Your Inner Selves choose a mutually acceptable solution that meets both their needs.

Through the idea generation process in Step Five, some solution or combination of ideas will evolve that both your Inner Parent and Inner Child can get excited about. This may be a best-of-both-worlds solution, as in the seminar vs. skiing example. Or it may be a situation which boils down to a choice between the lesser of two evils.

If all angles and creative ideas have mutually been explored, the solution or compromise will be agreed by both Inner Selves to be the best solution possible at that time.

Step Seven:

Your Inner Parent and Inner Child put the solution in motion.

This will be the easy part since both Selves had a hand in evolving the solution and are optimistic about the outcome.

Step Eight:
Both Selves evaluate the
solution for workability
and satisfaction.

Evaluate the success of your mutual endeavor.
Was the Self-Parenting solution to this Inner Conflict a
successful one? Was your Inner Child happy? Did the
compromise satisfy your Inner Parent? Could anything
be changed for the better next time? If the same
problem came up tomorrow, would you do anything
differently?

Use each experience of solving Inner Conflicts
to smooth out and pave the way for future problem-
solving.

The best method for heading off Inner Conflicts before they arise is to learn about and become more familiar with each Inner Self and its personality beforehand. Each Self is unique, with special needs and circumstances. As more and more conscious experience and interaction accumulates through practice of the Self-Parenting Exercises, your Inner Parent and Inner Child will get to know one another much more intimately.

As you, the Inner Parent, cooperate with you, the Inner Child, to resolve Inner Conflicts, a new confidence and trust will develop between your two Selves. Both will learn to be more open and aware of each other's needs. As in every successful relationship the two Inner Selves will grow in understanding and commitment as both learn to trust and depend on each other.

This self-confidence and self-mastery for finding mutual solutions acceptable to both Inner Selves will make each resolution of Inner Conflict progressively easier.

Through commitment and practice Win/Win solutions for your Inner Conflicts will become the norm.

When you, as an Inner Parent, consciously and actively work towards a Win/Win solution with your Inner Child, you will create a whole new perspective on life.

You will develop successful skills for living that will benefit you for the rest of your life. I advise you to start making room right now for all the happiness, love, and joy that you've always wanted and is now available to you.

SELF-
PARENTING
YOUR INNER
CONFLICTS:
YOUR FUTURE

The key to Self-Parenting is to resolve any Inner Conflicts you have by practicing and listening to *your* Inner Conversations.

> Do you have a weight problem?
>
> Are you unhappy or lonely?
>
> Do you have job-related stress?
>
> Are you having trouble deciding where to go to school or what to study?
>
> Are you getting a divorce or making decisions as to where to live or with whom?

These are serious situations or dilemmas. Listening to your Inner Conversations and practicing the Self-Parenting Exercises is the ideal way to work them out.

Although this book is written in a light and easy-to-read style, the principles underlying Self-Parenting in your Inner Conversations result from a sophisticated understanding of the human mind. Once you understand how you Inner Conversations influence your behavior, there are many applications for Self-Parenting which have long-term beneficial effects that can truly transform your life.

There are three levels or degrees of under-
standing the true value of Self-Parenting in your Inner
Conversations. These levels also represent the steps
you must take to unlock the treasures inside your mind
and to conquer past, present, and future challenges.

Level One Self-Parenting:
    **Learning to recognize the voices of your Inner
Conversations so you can separate the Inner Parent
from the Inner Child.**

Your thoughts, judgments, and analyses represent your Inner Parent.

Your feelings, emotions, and responses are your Inner Child.

These concepts are easy to understand intellectually but are so much harder to realize within your own mind. The leap from intellectual realization to emotional understanding and finally to practical application takes time and discipline. You have taken the first step, of course, by reading this book, and if practical, attending a Self-Parenting workshop.

For many people the idea of having Inner Conversations is a new one. Others may have intuitively heard their Inner Conversations during the day. But since they did not know who the participants were, they never really "listened" to what was actually being said. Their Inner Parent unconcsciously Self-Parented their Inner Child in the same manner in which they were raised.

Level One Self-Parenting of Inner Conversations is similar to reading about a new program of physical exercises. Discovering a better and easier way to exercise can inspire you to think about exercising. Yet, even if you like and understand the reasoning behind the "how and why" to exercise, if you don't actually practice the new exercises you won't get the benefits. By the same principle, until you practice the Self-Parenting Exercises in Part III you will remain at Level One understanding.

Others may have the attitude, "I know all about this, I studied it years ago in a psychology class," or "I read a book about something like that." However, attaining intellectual realization (Level One understanding) is only the first step to achieving the self-actualization that is possible. You will discover going beyond Level One into Level Two to be much more emotionally satisfying.

Level Two Self-Parenting:
Getting to know your Inner Child

You get to know your Inner Child by practicing the Self-Parenting Exercises.

Starting with the first session you will begin to separate the two voices inside your mind so that each side can be heard more clearly. You will also start to establish your own style of creative Self-Parenting dialogue.

By practicing just thirty minutes a day you will quickly discover something really unique.

There truly is an Inner Child voice with its own perspective and viewpoints. This voice is above and beyond what you most likely assumed while reading this book. Two to four weeks of half-hour sessions are usually necessary to begin realizing exceptional progress.

As you accumulate half-hour sessions a deeper and more magical awareness of your Inner Conversations takes place. Soon you will tap into the power and beauty inherent within these concepts, and Level Three understanding will come about as a natural extension of getting to know your Inner Child.

Level Three Self-Parenting:

Changing any patterns of negative Inner Parenting to positive patterns of loving, supporting, and nurturing yourself.

Level Three Self-Parenting is understanding your Inner Conversations well enough to use them on an ongoing, daily basis, to love, support, and nurture yourself.

At Level Three you will discover that you don't really have many outer problems at all. You mostly have Inner Conflicts that remain unresolved simply because you haven't addressed the issues at their source—inside your mind.

The entrenchment of longstanding negative parental programming may be too solid to excavate on your own. The psychological patterns which develop from unusually harsh parenting (such as by parents who were alcoholics) can be too subtle or deep to see from Level One or even Level Two awareness. Your early childhood experiences (and thus the voice of your Inner Child) may be too painful to uncover and can be literally blocked from your awareness. In these circumstances it takes a trained professional (see Part III, Chapter 12) to gently clarify your Inner Conversations and lead you to more positive Self-Parenting. Most of us, however, are unfulfilled or unhappy because we simply are not taking the time needed to love, support, and nurture ourselves in the most aware and knowledgeable manner possible.

CONCLUSION

Don't be content with Level One awareness of your Inner Conversations. Practice the Self-Parenting Exercises in Part III. Seek the deeper awareness of how your mind works. Once you achieve Level Three awareness, use your half-hour Self-Parenting sessions to crack open the psychic barriers between you and the powers of your mind. Your potential as a human being is awe inspiring. Start living up to it!

Happiness, fulfillment, and meaning in your life are the natural consequences of positive, loving, and nurturing Self-Parenting.

It is a very widespread syndrome to look for a Self-Parenting substitute outside of our Inner Conversations, something or someone else to care for and understand our needs and to take responsibility for our lives.

Unfortunately, if our physical, emotional, mental, and social needs are not met from within our own Selves and our family support system, they will never truly be met from a more distant source such as a job, possessions, or society.

The best source of loving, supporting, and nurturing is the one you control, positive Self-Parenting within your own Inner Conversations.

The most important aspect of your Inner Conversations is that you actually Self-Parent your Inner Child. Don't just learn or read about it; practice to genuinely build yourself up when you feel emotionally depressed, afraid, bored, or angry.

Use Self-Parenting as a tool to fix yourself up when you are really down.

Use your Inner Conversations for self-nurturing and meeting your own needs rather than hoping for possessions or other people from "out there" to provide them.

When parents properly nurture an outer child it grows up with a powerful sense of self-esteem, self-respect, and an intuitive experience of its own connection to others. A completely nurtured child is capable of everything and anything. When this child becomes an adult, there are no obstacles to he or she achieving whatever is wanted in life.

By reestablishing this same foundation through positive Self-Parenting in your Inner Conversations, you will achieve the same, positive results. You will gradually uncover and eliminate negative aspects of your Inner Child and change them to the positive. Soon you will find your Inner Child becoming more self-sufficient, more dependable, more reliable, and more responsible. The energy your Inner Selves wasted fighting each other can now be magnified with double the power to attain your mutual goals.

Self-Parenting is an intensive method for achieving self-actualization. By doing your half-hour sessions properly and staying with them you can achieve almost anything. After several months of Level Three Self-Parenting, your Inner Parent and Inner Child will become truly cooperative and completely nurtured. You will become a very powerful person able to make miracles happen in your life.

It's never too late to make your life work just the way you've always desired.

You can also use Self-Parenting as a counseling tool with others. It's a wonderful understanding to share with your friends. Compare and contrast what their Inner Parent and Inner Child are saying. Notice where they have become stuck by repeating non-nurturing behavior learned from their parents. Your experience and knowledge can assist them in loving, supporting, and nurturing the needs of their Inner Selves.

Your relationship with your Inner Child is the only relationship you can be absolutely certain will be with you for the rest of your life. You and your Inner Child will be having Inner Conversations for as long as you live.

If you start Self-Parenting now with love, nurturing, and support, your future can only be brighter and more fulfilling.

I wish you the greatest success in learning, understanding, and working with your Inner Conversations. I know you have gotten to know your Inner Child more and I hope you will continue to study how to love, support, and nurture him or her.

I would be very happy to hear about your personal experiences listening to your Inner Conversations and with Self-Parenting. Write to me if you would like to share an intense Inner Conversation you have resolved or to tell me how positively Self-Parenting in your Inner Conversations has benefited your life. [Publisher's note: If a personal reply is requested, please include a self-addressed, stamped envelope.] Your response (and that of your Inner Child) may become a part of my next book, *The Self-Parenting Manual: More About Your Inner Conversations*. Good luck!

Dr. John Pollard
c/o Generic Human Studies Publishing
P.O. Box 6466-A
Malibu, CA 90265

PART III
SELF-PARENTING EXERCISES

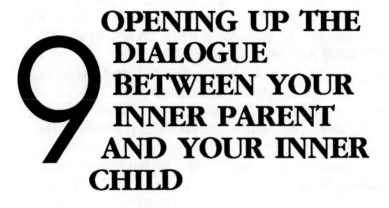

9 OPENING UP THE DIALOGUE BETWEEN YOUR INNER PARENT AND YOUR INNER CHILD

INTRODUCTION

You are now familiar with the two voices inside your mind: your Inner Parent and your Inner Child. You also know how to Self-Parent when you encounter Inner Conflicts. The next step of positive Self-Parenting is to become more aware of your Inner Conversations. Start tuning into them to discover which voice is which. **YOUR INNER CONVERSATIONS ARE GOING ON ALL THE TIME!**

To gain the positive benefits of Self-Parenting your Inner Parent has the primary responsibility for studying and developing your Inner Conversations. Part III will outline the steps to assist you in this process. The first two chapters will teach you the format of the Self-Parenting sessions and how to recognize the voice of your Inner Child. Chapter 11 will give you ideas on how to use your Self-Parenting sessions to improve the practical conditions in your life. Chapter 12 will give you further references to develop Level III, Self-Parenting in the "real world."

You, as the Inner Parent, must practice if you want to Self-Parent your Inner Child in a nurturing and supportive way. This process is initiated in the same way outer parents might correct problems with their outer child. Let's suppose that two parents are experiencing a lack of communication with their son and he is turning into a difficult disciplinary problem.

One day the parents read a book or attend a lecture on effective parenting techniques and are exposed to new ideas or methods they never knew existed. As a result the parents realize the problems with their child are actually the result of poor parenting skills rather than any fault of the child's. Until now the parents have unknowingly been using non-nurturing parenting techniques. So, they decide to change methods immediately.

Changing their normal parenting style immediately will prove difficult however, because now the parents have a brand new problem. They have only just learned the new and different parenting techniques and they will have to practice these new methods a while before gaining proficiency. Also, since the child is being exposed to a radical new parenting style he may become even more rebellious. All he knows is he hasn't liked the style of parenting he has received until now, so why should a new approach be any different?

Yet, through practicing the new parenting style with consistency, the parents gain new skills and confidence. As the child begins to experience the benefits of better parenting, he responds with a different attitude. As a result of the initial study and changes made by the parents and the changing response of the child, the relationship between them gradually and permanently improves.

In the same way, you (the Inner Parent) are responsible for correcting your half of the Inner Conversations first. As your Inner Parent starts Self-Parenting properly, the response from your Inner Child will naturally positive.

You fulfill your Self-Parenting duties by learning the generic principles and dynamics of the Inner Conversations as well as by developing ways to personalize and implement these new concepts into your daily life. You must unlearn the bad habits that you perpetuate from your parents as well as develop new methods and techniques for positive Self-Parenting within your Inner Conversations.

The initial energy for change, provided by your Inner Parent, will carry this plan of action far enough for both of you to get a taste of the Inner Child's ENTHUSIASM! Once the positive benefits of working with your Inner Conversations are gained, the two Selves will continue to motivate each other. As the Inner Parent and Inner Child improve their relationship through daily half-hour sessions, the momentum and excitement for positive Self-Parenting builds rapidly.

The Self-Parenting Exercises provide the next step for the gaining of these benefits. To begin this process your Inner Parent starts by paying conscious attention to the voice of your Inner Child. This half-hour session is a commitment by your Inner Parent to provide you and your Inner Child undisturbed access to each other so you can get to know each other better.

During the first week the goal for the Self-Parenting sessions is for you, the Inner Parent, to simply start listening for and getting to know the voice of your Inner Child more clearly. As you become more conscious of what your Inner Child wants and needs you can use positive Self-Parenting techniques and methods to build a more mutually nurturing relationship. If you start doing the advanced exercises before establishing a relationship with your Inner Child, the Inner Child will not feel safe enough to participate and your sessions together will be ineffective.

To explore deeper levels of your Inner Conversations I recommend the following procedure. This is the method taught by the Self-Parenting teachers and it has proven very successful for students practicing these daily sessions.

STEP 1
ESTABLISHING THE SETTING

Establish a comfortable setting in which your daily Self-Parenting sessions can take place. Make every effort to have your sessions at the same time and place each day. Many types of settings are possible depending on the likes and dislikes of your Inner Parent and Inner Child. The most successful time for the Self-Parenting students has been in the morning after waking up. The most convenient time for you to Self-Parent may be after you wake up, at lunch, or just about any time as long as it is consistent and both Selves are comfortable.

As an Inner Parent, you do not want distractions such as the television, radio, work, or phone calls to pull your attention away from your Inner Child. One caution however, this is not meditation with "closed eyes in a darkened room." The ideal situation is a quiet environment with moderate lighting. You should be sitting up, alert and wide-awake. Both Selves need conscious concentration to participate in this process.

Provide a pen, some notebook paper, and a surface for writing down the responses of your Inner Child. Use separate sheets of paper for each half-hour session. I recommend that you save these written session responses in a binder.

Keeping a chronological record of your sessions enables you to work with others to improve the Self-Parenting of your Inner Child. Many therapists will actively help you sort out problems you are having, or you may attend a Self-Parenting workshop. Perhaps you are involved in a twelve-step program in which you can share these sessions with others to help work through trouble areas. To gain the benefits of therapy and evaluation of your Self-Parenting sessions, having them written down is a must.

Begin each half-hour session with a standard introduction, as the Inner Child loves consistent methods and procedures. This also gives a clear indication to your Inner Child that you are starting the session and tells it what you want to do. The standard introduction also allows the Inner Child psychological time to prepare for the session.

When you are comfortable and have prepared yourself for not being disturbed, start your session with the following introduction. Read it out loud to your Inner Child just as if you were talking to another person in the room.

Dear Inner Child,

Good morning (or afternoon) to you. I, as your Inner Parent, want to spend the next half-hour or so with you in order to get to know you better.

Knowing you and learning more about you is very important to me. I would like you, the Inner Child, and me, the Inner Parent, to understand and enjoy each other more completely. If you and I can learn to communicate more openly with each other and understand each other better, then we will both be happier.

I am going to ask you questions about things you know and feel so that I can learn more about your personality, feelings, and opinions. Feel free to answer these questions as simply or as completely as you like. My goal during this half-hour session is to listen to you as best as I can without judging or criticizing what you tell me. I really do want to get to know you and your viewpoints better.

I also would like you to know that even though I will be trying my best to listen without judging or criticizing, I know that I will probably make some mistakes. Since I know this, I apologize right now in advance. As soon as I become aware that I am not listening to you objectively I will apologize again and go back to listening to your answers as best as I can. Thank you for your cooperation.

The one who wants to know you best,

Your Inner Parent

STEP 2
ASKING QUESTIONS

The next step of positive Self-Parenting is simply for the Inner Parent to start asking the Inner Child some "door-opener" type questions. Ask these questions using this format:

"Inner Child, _____?"

Speak these questions firmly and out loud, as if you were talking to another person. Then, let go of your Inner Parent mind and listen in a quiet way for the answers from your Inner Child. You will hear your questions being answered inside your mind as thoughts or mental impressions. *This is the voice of your Inner Child responding to your questions!*

A key principle of the Self-Parenting sessions is that when you are speaking aloud you are using the voice of your Inner Parent. The Inner Child voice is represented by your thoughts. By artificially separating the two Inner Selves using this technique, you will be able to differentiate the two voices more easily.

For many of you this process will be very easy. The questions you ask will elicit strong responses and your Inner Child will start giving you answers straight away. Sometimes the answers may be short or slow in coming, especially if you have suppressed your Inner Child for many years. Don't worry if you don't hear anything immediately. Sometimes it takes a while for your Inner Child to catch on and trust what you are doing. The Inner Parent can also be confused about the technique. Either way, practice makes perfect.

As an Inner Parent you might read over the questions and think to yourself, "Boy, this is stupid. I know all the answers to these questions already." This attitude is one of the main problems with the Inner Parent. It thinks it knows all the answers. The Self-Parenting sessions work best when you ask these questions of the Inner Child with a fresh attitude, as if to a complete stranger.

At other times the Inner Child's response may be surprisingly intense and emotional. **DON'T WORRY IF THE ANSWERS FROM YOUR INNER CHILD ARE STRONGLY INTENSE OR DIFFERENT FROM WHAT YOU** (the Inner Parent) **MIGHT HAVE THOUGHT THEM TO BE.** Your Inner Child is a different personality than your Inner Parent. A different answer from what you might have expected *is a sure sign that your Inner Child is actually talking to you.*

STEP 3
WRITING DOWN THE INNER CHILD'S RESPONSE

After you have asked your Inner Child a question, write down the thoughts that come into your mind. You will write down the responses of your Inner Child as part of your Self-Parenting session for two reasons. One is to have a permanent record of your Inner Child's answers to your questions. Another reason is that writing down the responses of the Inner Child is a crucial aspect of the positive Self-Parenting process.

For example, suppose you ask your Inner Child out loud the following question:

"Inner Child, how are you doing today?"

In your mind you will hear thoughts or feel mental impressions such as:

"I am doing fine."
"My head hurts."
"I'm tired."
"I'm excited to be doing this."
"I'm uncomfortable sitting in this chair."
"I'm not sure what you want me to say."
"I'm nervous."

This is the voice of your Inner Child responding to your question.

When writing down the responses of your Inner Child it is important to use what is called the **"You're feeling that..."** format. Using the **"You're feeling that..."** format serves the very important function of separating the thoughts of your Inner Parent from the feelings of your Inner Child. As you hear or feel the responses of your Inner Child inside your mind, write them down in the following manner:

"You're feeling that you're doing fine."
"You're feeling that your head hurts."
"You're feeling that you are tired."
"You're feeling that you are excited to be doing this."
"You're feeling that you are uncomfortable sitting in this chair."
"You're feeling that you are not sure what I want you to say."
"You're feeling that you are nervous."

Your Inner Child may talk briefly and have nothing more to say or it may go on and on. In the beginning it may be shy or confused. Your Inner Child may want to give you a response it thinks you want to hear, rather than realizing that you actually want it to tell you what it thinks. During these beginning sessions evaluate the response time of your Inner Child as if you were in a conversation with a friend. Don't leave a question too soon if, as the Inner Parent, you feel the Inner Child may want to communicate more information. On the other hand, don't let mental silence drag out too long. Your initial Self-Parenting sessions may require some timing adjustments for both Inner Selves.

Whatever your Inner Child says—it is important for you to write down the responses with the parroting technique of **"You're feeling that."** During the first week's sessions you must establish a strong separation between the questions of your Inner Parent and the responses of your Inner Child. You simply and only want to write the Inner Child's responses, using the same words that it uses.

A frequent problem during the beginning Self-Parenting sessions is negative feedback coming automatically from the Inner Parent—judging, commenting, or in some way interfering with what the Inner Child says. For example, in response to a question such as who it likes the most, your Inner Child may give an answer your Inner Parent thinks is preposterous. Or there may be negative opinions and emotions coming from your Inner Child that take your Inner Parent completely by surprise. Before you know it, your Inner Parent thinks twelve negative thoughts to the one honest response of your Inner Child.

Instead of reacting negatively (or positively, for that matter) to the answers, simply repeat whatever your Inner Child says and write it down using the **"You're feeling that..."** format. You will know when you are judging positively or negatively by the extra thoughts in your head which are not a response to your question, but are mental feedback to the responses of the Inner Child. They will be parental sounding judgments or advice such as good/bad, right/wrong, or better/worse.

When you do have Inner Parent thoughts or judgments (and you will) don't worry, because everyone does at first; it is unavoidable. In fact, during your standard introduction, you have even apologized to your Inner Child in advance for this very problem! Just remember the following. When you do find yourself arguing, judging, or thinking that the response of your Inner Child is "wrong," or "stupid," be sure to **STOP** right away and **APOLOGIZE** again by saying out loud:

> **"I'm sorry, Inner Child. I was judging what you told me. Please go ahead with what you were saying before I interrupted. I'll keep practicing not to do this in the future."**

Remember, your job as the Inner Parent during these sessions is to be the receiver and reflect like a mirror what the Inner Child is saying. Your Inner Child must feel more safe and secure answering questions during your Self-Parenting sessions than at any other time of the day. The strange and unusual answers you get will help you discover more and more about your Inner Child's thoughts, feelings, and needs, which of course, is the purpose of the Self-Parenting sessions in the first place.

ACCEPT THE ANSWERS OF THE INNER CHILD DURING THESE SESSIONS WITHOUT JUDGMENTS! During the first two weeks, you (the Inner Parent) never want to judge or condemn anything your Inner Child says, even if your Inner Parent knows it to be completely wrong. In following weeks of Self-Parenting sessions, your Inner Parent will have the opportunity to talk back to your Inner Child.

The worst thing you can do during the initial Self-Parenting Exercises is to impose your old parental patterns on your Inner Child or stop the session because your Inner Parent doesn't like what your Inner Child says. If you do this you will upset your Inner Child because you have judged it critically for giving an answer that you, the Inner Parent, requested in the first place. This would be similar to an outer parent punishing a child for telling the truth. The outer child quickly learns not to tell the truth, and in the same manner your Inner Child will quickly learn not to respond to your questions.

STEP 4
THANK YOUR INNER CHILD FOR ITS RESPONSE

After you have recorded the full response of your Inner Child, be sure to thank it for answering you openly and honestly. Do this after each question. Direct the following statement inward to your Inner Child and remember to say it out loud:

"Thank you, Inner Child, for telling me that."

Thanking your Inner Child after each question allows it to feel happy and secure since, for the first time, it is being heard and accepted without judgment or disapproval. The Inner Parent's question, the Inner Child's response, followed by a positive acknowledgment from the Inner Parent, begins the loving, supporting, and nurturing that is such an important part of Self-Parenting. This alone will start to build positive "points" with your Inner Child which will contribute to your well-being throughout your day.

STEP 5
END THE SESSION

The ideal Self-Parenting question and answer session is a half-hour. It's not important how fast you proceed through these questions or even if you complete all of them in one session. What is important is that you, as the Inner Parent, have taken the full half-hour out of your busy schedule to love, support, and nurture your Inner Child.

On the other hand, you and your Inner Child could start having such a good time that neither of you wants to stop and you might find your first session going overtime. It's recommended that you do not give in to this tempting pleasure. Limiting session times to only a half-hour has given our Self-Parenting students the best overall results.

It is the accrued consistency of the Self-Parenting sessions that brings benefits to your daily life. A session that goes on too long in the beginning causes your Inner Child to feel too exhilarated or invigorated. Since you feel so good, you wind up skipping your session for a few days. It then becomes much harder to start up again because you have lost your positive momentum. There is also a feeling of betrayal on the part of your Inner Child who feels that the Inner Parent started something good and then dropped it.

So, after thirty minutes it is time to end the session. Again, use a standard closing. This lets your Inner Child know that the session is over and also contributes to their consistency. The following statement works well as a closing.

Dear Inner Child,

It has been a half-hour now since we have been talking and sharing with each other. I really have enjoyed it and I feel grateful that we could spend this time together. Tomorrow let's do it again and have just as much fun. (You might also include some special words of appreciation specific to the session.)

Thanks again,

Your Inner Parent

Repeat this process of asking questions, writing down the responses, and thanking the Inner Child for approximately thirty minutes each day. As a result, you will start hearing **YOUR** Inner Child with a much clearer and much stronger voice during the rest of your daily activities.

The following questions are a suggested schedule for the first week's Self-Parenting sessions. I strongly recommend that you follow the half-hour format using these beginning questions. The initial goal for Self-Parenting sessions during the first week is to simply establish a consistent amount of time each day to love, support, and nurture your Inner Child. This will demonstrate in a concrete way to your Inner Child that you, as the Inner Parent, are serious about changing your previous Self-Parenting patterns.

Practicing the proper form and demonstrating to your Inner Child that you actively want to get to know it better will accomplish wonders for your relationship. This is the most important benefit of the first week of Self-Parenting. You and your Inner Child need this time to reestablish the bond you once shared. These questions will gently and easily allow your Inner Child to safely express non-threatening answers to non-threatening questions in a non-threatening environment.

DAY ONE

Some beginning questions that you can use are:

1. Inner Child, how are you doing today?
   You're feeling that:

2. Inner Child, do you think it's strange to have these Self-Parenting sessions?
   You're feeling that:

3. Inner Child, are you feeling comfortable right now?
   You're feeling that:

4. Inner Child, how did you sleep last night?
   You're feeling that:

5. Inner Child, what did you eat for breakfast this morning (or dinner last night)?
   You're feeling that:

6. Inner Child, did you enjoy the meal?
   You're feeling that:

7. Inner Child, what are your three favorite foods?
   You're feeling that:

8. When did you last get to eat each of your three favorite foods?
   You're feeling that:

9. Inner Child, what is your favorite movie?
   You're feeling that:

10. Inner Child, what is it about that movie that you like so much?
    You're feeling that:

11. Inner Child, who is your favorite actor/actress?
    You're feeling that:

12. Inner Child, what is it about that actor/actress that you like so much?
    You're feeling that:

13. Inner Child, tell me about something you did today (or yesterday) that you enjoyed.
    You're feeling that:

14. Inner Child, tell me about something you did today (or yesterday) that you didn't enjoy.
    You're feeling that:

15. Inner Child, is there anything else you would like to tell me before we end this session?
    You're feeling that:

DAY TWO

1. Inner Child, how are you feeling today?
    You're feeling that:

2. Inner Child, how is your physical body feeling right now?
    You're feeling that:

3. Inner Child, what is your emotional state right now?
    You're feeling that:

4. Inner Child, what is your favorite kind of music?
    You're feeling that:

5. Inner Child, who is your favorite singer or musical group?
    You're feeling that:

6. Inner Child, when was the last time you heard your favorite music?
    You're feeling that:

7. Inner Child, how many albums do you have by that singer/group?
    You're feeling that:

8. Inner Child, would you like to have more albums by that singer/group?
    You're feeling that:

9. Inner Child, tell me about something you did today (or yesterday) that you enjoyed.
You're feeling that:

10. Inner Child, tell me about something you did today (or yesterday) that you didn't enjoy.
You're feeling that:

11. Inner Child, what did you eat for lunch (today or yesterday)?
You're feeling that:

12. Inner Child, what was your favorite part of the meal?
You're feeling that:

13. Inner Child, what was your least favorite part of the meal?
You're feeling that:

14. Inner Child, what is another one of your favorite movies that you didn't tell me yesterday?
You're feeling that:

15. Inner Child, what was it you enjoyed most about that movie?
You're feeling that:

16. Inner Child, is there anything else you would like to tell me before we end this session?
You're feeling that:

DAY THREE

1. Inner Child, how are you feeling today?
   You're feeling that:

2. Inner Child, are you comfortable?
   You're feeling that:

3. Inner Child, how do you like doing these Self-Parenting sessions?
   You're feeling that:

4. Inner Child, what would you like to make you feel more comfortable during these sessions?
   You're feeling that:

5. Inner Child, how did you sleep last night?
   You're feeling that:

6. Inner Child, were you comfortable when you slept last night?
   You're feeling that:

7. Inner Child, what is your favorite sport to play?
   You're feeling that:

8. When did you last exercise or play your favorite sport?
   You're feeling that:

9. If you could be any athlete, who would it be?
   You're feeling that:

10. What is it about that athlete that you like so much?
    You're feeling that:

11. Inner Child, if you had your choice, what would you like for dinner?
    You're feeling that:

12. Inner Child, if you had your choice, who would you like to talk to on the phone?
    You're feeling that:

13. Inner Child, what person do you love the most in the world?
    You're feeling that:

14. Inner Child, what person do you hate the most in the world?
    You're feeling that:

15. Inner Child, is there anything else you would like to tell me before we end this session?
    You're feeling that:

DAY FOUR

1. Inner Child, how are you doing today?
    You're feeling that:

2. Inner Child, how is your physical body feeling right now?
    You're feeling that:

3. Inner Child, what is your emotional state right now?
    You're feeling that:

4. Inner Child, which room is your favorite where you live?
    You're feeling that:

5. Inner Child, what is it about that room that you like so much?
    You're feeling that:

6. Inner Child, which room is your least favorite where you live?
    You're feeling that:

7. Inner Child, what is it about that room that you dislike so much?
    You're feeling that:

8. Inner Child, what would make that room a better room to be in?
    You're feeling that:

9. Inner Child, can you remember a time when you were sad?
   You're feeling that:

10. Inner Child, tell me about that time.
    You're feeling that:

11. Inner Child, can you remember a time when you were happy?
    You're feeling that:

12. Inner Child, tell me about that time.
    You're feeling that:

13. Inner Child, who is your favorite male friend?
    You're feeling that:

14. Inner Child, what makes him your favorite special male friend?
    You're feeling that:

15. Inner Child, is there anything else you would like to tell me before we end this session?
    You're feeling that:

DAY FIVE

1. Inner Child, how are you feeling today?
   You're feeling that:

2. Inner Child, are you feeling comfortable?
   You're feeling that:

3. Inner Child, what kinds of things do you like to do for fun?
   You're feeling that:

4. Inner Child, why do you like to do those things so much?
   You're feeling that:

5. Inner Child, when was the last time you got to do those things?
   You're feeling that:

6. Inner Child, what is your favorite possession?
   You're feeling that:

7. Inner Child, how would you feel if you lost your favorite possession?
   You're feeling that:

8. Inner Child, who is your favorite female friend?
   You're feeling that:

9. Inner Child, what makes her your favorite special female friend?
You're feeling that:

10. Inner Child, can you remember a recent time when you were enthusiastic and energetic?
You're feeling that:

11. Inner Child, what made you so enthusiastic and energetic?
You're feeling that:

12. Inner Child, can you remember a recent time when you received a gift?
You're feeling that:

13. Inner Child, how did receiving that gift make you feel?
You're feeling that:

14. Inner Child, can you remember a time when you got a pet?
You're feeling that:

15. Inner Child, is there anything else you would like to tell me before we end this session?
You're feeling that:

DAY SIX

1. Inner Child, how are you feeling today?
    You're feeling that:

2. Inner Child, how is your physical body feeling right now?
    You're feeling that:

3. Inner Child, how is your emotional state right now?
    You're feeling that:

4. Inner Child, can you remember a time you went swimming?
    You're feeling that:

5. Inner Child, can you remember an earlier time you went swimming?
    You're feeling that:

6. Inner Child, when was your favorite vacation?
    You're feeling that:

7. Inner Child, what did you do on that vacation that was the most fun?
    You're feeling that:

8. Inner Child, what else did you do on that vacation that was fun?
    You're feeling that:

9. Inner Child, what famous person do you really admire?
   You're feeling that:

10. Inner Child, what do you admire most about that famous person?
    You're feeling that:

11. Inner Child, can you remember a famous event that you really thought was important?
    You're feeling that:

12. Inner Child, how did that event affect you personally?
    You're feeling that:

13. Inner Child, can you tell me about a time when you were angry?
    You're feeling that:

14. Inner Child, can you tell me about a time when you felt confident?
    You're feeling that:

15. Inner Child, is there anything else you would like to tell me before we end this session?
    You're feeling that:

DAY SEVEN

1. Inner Child, how are you doing today?
   You're feeling that:

2. Inner Child, are you comfortable?
   You're feeling that:

3. Inner Child, can you remember a time when you felt afraid?
   You're feeling that:

4. Inner Child, tell me more about that experience.
   You're feeling that:

5. Inner Child, can you remember a time when you created or made something?
   You're feeling that:

6. Inner Child, what was it?
   You're feeling that:

7. Inner Child, how did creating it make you feel?
   You're feeling that:

8. Inner Child, can you remember a time when got something you wanted?
   You're feeling that:

9. Inner Child, what was it?
   You're feeling that:

10. Inner Child, why were you glad to get it?
    You're feeling that:

11. Inner Child, can you remember a time when you didn't
    get something you wanted?
    You're feeling that:

12. Inner Child, why were you upset that you didn't get it?
    You're feeling that:

13. Inner Child, can you remember a time when you got
    something you didn't want?
    You're feeling that:

14. Inner Child, why were you unhappy to get it?
    You're feeling that:

15. Inner Child, is there anything else you would like to tell
    me before we end this session?
    You're feeling that:

10 ADVANCING THE SELF-PARENTING EXERCISES

INTRODUCTION

After following the initial Self-Parenting sessions for a week, you and your Inner Child are much more in tune with each other. Now the introductory questions will be less interesting for both of you. One way to advance the sessions is to encourage your Inner Child to go back into its memories.

One particular aspect of the Inner Child is that it functions as the gatekeeper to the memory storehouse. Only the Inner Child can have memories (just as only the Inner Child can feel the emotions). To recall a memory, it is necessary for the Inner Parent to request the Inner Child to bring up or replay that memory. Once your Inner Child makes the recall, it then feeds the memory into your Inner Conversation. The Inner Child can also have spontaneous recall due to outer stimuli. Familiar sights, pictures, and especially smells stir up old memories within your Inner Child.

One method of deepening the sessions and aiding memory recall is to have a favorite picture of you as a child at the session. This picture should be a happy one that evokes fond memories or has an obviously happy expression. Directing your questions to your Inner Child with this picture present helps your Inner Child recall feelings and events of the past.

When asking the Inner Child to recall memories it can sometimes take a while for the Inner Child to come up with something. Other times it will remember incidents or feelings so quickly your Inner Parent will be flabbergasted. It may also be helpful to close your eyes to reduce outer stimulation when asking your Inner Child to recall memories.

Another method of deepening the sessions is to ask your Inner Child more intimate questions. These would be questions of a strictly personal nature between you and your Inner Child involving feelings about family problems, work ethics, sexual situations, religious matters. Also, asking your Inner Child "why" questions will elicit deeper (and more powerful) emotions as it begins to feel safer and more at ease. "Why" questions also allow your Inner Child to freely volunteer feelings on its own terms, the way it wants to reveal them.

Always remember when asking questions to use the **"You're feeling that"** formula to keep the opinions and thoughts of your Inner Child separate from that of your Inner Parent. Also remember to keep your Self-Parenting sessions to thirty minutes and follow this simple procedure:

1. Establish the setting.

2. Ask the questions out loud using the "Inner Child,..." format.

3. Write down the Inner Child's responses exactly using the **"You're feeling that"** formula.

4. After each question is fully answered, thank the Inner Child out loud.

5. End the session after thirty minutes.

The questions of the second week are designed to stimulate your Inner Child to bring up deeper emotions or past memories during your Self-Parenting sessions. These questions and others like them will stimulate your Inner Child to tell you volumes of interesting things that will keep both of you fascinated during your daily Self-Parenting half-hour. If you are interested in other lines of questioning you may make up your own questions.

DAY EIGHT

1. Inner Child, how are you feeling today?
   You're feeling that:

2. Inner Child, why are you feeling that way?
   You're feeling that:

3. Inner Child, what do you remember liking most about school?
   You're feeling that:

4. Inner Child, is there anything else you liked about school?
   You're feeling that:

5. Inner Child, do you remember a particular incident that you truly enjoyed?
   You're feeling that:

6. Inner Child, what do you remember hating most about school?
   You're feeling that:

7. Inner Child, why did you hate that so much?
   You're feeling that:

8. Inner Child, do you remember any particular incident that you truly hated?
   You're feeling that:

9. Inner Child, what are some of your favorite activities you'd like to do soon?
   You're feeling that:

10. Inner Child, why do you enjoy them so much?
    You're feeling that:

11. Inner Child, when was the last time you got to do them?
    You're feeling that:

12. Inner Child, when was the very first time you enjoyed
    the activity?
    You're feeling that:

13. Inner Child, do you like nature?
    You're feeling that:

14. Inner Child, what type of environment in nature do you
    like best?
    You're feeling that:

15. Inner Child, what is your favorite weather condition:
    rain, clouds, snow, thunder, sun, wind, day, night, cold,
    hot, moderate, dawn, sunset, noon, hail, stars, moon,
    dew, fog?
    You're feeling that:

16. Inner Child, how does that weather condition make you
    feel?
    You're feeling that:

17. Inner Child, is there anything else you would like to tell
    me before we end this session?
    You're feeling that:

DAY NINE

1. Inner Child, how are you feeling today?
   You're feeling that:

2. Inner Child, how is your physical body feeling right now?
   You're feeling that:

3. Inner Child, what part of your body feels the tightest?
   You're feeling that:

4. Inner Child, what part of your body feels the most relaxed?
   You're feeling that:

5. Inner Child, what is your favorite book?
   You're feeling that:

6. Inner Child, why did you like that book so much?
   You're feeling that:

7. Inner Child, how long has it been since you read it or a book that good?
   You're feeling that:

8. Inner Child, on a scale of 1-to-10 how much do you like to read?
   You're feeling that:

9. Inner Child, do you remember a time as a child when you were enthusiastic and energetic?
   You're feeling that:

10. Inner Child, how old were you at the time?
    You're feeling that:

11. Inner Child, tell me more about that time.
    You're feeling that:

12. Inner Child, when was the last time you felt that good?
    You're feeling that:

13. Inner Child, can you remember a birthday between the ages of five and ten?
    You're feeling that:

14. Inner Child, tell me about that birthday.
    You're feeling that:

15. Inner Child, can you remember a gift you received?
    You're feeling that:

16. Inner Child, how did receiving that gift make you feel inside?
    You're feeling that:

17. Inner Child, is there anything else you would like to tell me before we end this session?
    You're feeling that:

DAY TEN

1. Inner Child, how are you feeling today?
    You're feeling that:

2. Inner Child, what is your emotional state right now?
    You're feeling that:

3. Inner Child, can you remember a time as a child when you were bored or depressed?
    You're feeling that:

4. Inner Child, how old were you at the time?
    You're feeling that:

5. Inner Child, tell me about that time.
    You're feeling that:

6. Inner Child, when was the last time you felt that bad?
    You're feeling that:

7. Inner Child, do you remember a time as a child when you were enthusiastic and energetic?
    You're feeling that:

8. Inner Child, how old were you at the time?
    You're feeling that:

9. Inner Child, tell me more about that time.
    You're feeling that:

10. Inner Child, can you remember a Christmas between the ages of five and ten?
    You're feeling that:

11. Inner Child, tell me about that Christmas.
You're feeling that:

12. Inner Child, what person in your life do you love the most?
You're feeling that:

13. Inner Child, what are the traits that make you love him or her?
You're feeling that:

14. Inner Child, what person in your life do you hate the most?
You're feeling that:

15. Inner Child, what traits about that person make you hate him or her?
You're feeling that:

16. Inner Child, can you remember a time as a child when you did someone a favor?
You're feeling that:

17. Inner Child, tell me about that.
You're feeling that:

18. Inner Child, how did doing that favor make you feel inside?
You're feeling that:

19. Inner Child, is there anything else you would like to tell me before we end this session?
You're feeling that:

DAY ELEVEN

1. Inner Child, how are you feeling right now?
    You're feeling that:

2. Inner Child, are you feeling better physically or emotionally?
    You're feeling that:

3. Inner Child, tell me why you feel that way?
    You're feeling that:

4. Inner Child, approximately ten years ago (or 20, 30, 40) what specific event or incident really made you happy?
    You're feeling that:

5. Inner Child, why did that event make you feel so good?
    You're feeling that:

6. Inner Child, approximately ten years ago (or 20, 30, 40) what specific event or incident really made you feel bad?
    You're feeling that:

7. Inner Child, what was it about that event that made you feel so bad?
    You're feeling that:

8. Inner Child, what is your favorite color?
    You're feeling that:

9. Inner Child, how many clothes do you have in that color?
    You're feeling that:

10. Inner Child, how do you feel about the clothes we wear?
    You're feeling that:

11. Inner Child, if you had your choice, what would you change about our clothes?
You're feeling that:

12. Inner Child, can you tell me about a time when you needed help?
You're feeling that:

13. Inner Child, can you remember a time when you helped a friend?
You're feeling that:

14. Inner Child, what felt good about helping your friend?
You're feeling that:

15. Inner Child, in the last week what specific event or incident really made you happy?
You're feeling that:

16. Inner Child, why did that event make you feel so good?
You're feeling that:

17. Inner Child, in the last week what specific event or incident really made you feel bad?
You're feeling that:

18. Inner Child, what about that event made you feel so bad?
You're feeling that:

19. Inner Child, is there anything else you would like to tell me before we end this session?
You're feeling that:

DAY TWELVE

1. Inner Child, how is your physical body feeling right now?
    You're feeling that:

2. Inner Child, what is your emotional state right now?
    You're feeling that:

3. Inner Child, what would you like to feel more comfortable?
    You're feeling that:

4. Inner Child, who was your favorite teacher in college (high school, primary school)?
    You're feeling that:

5. Inner Child, why did you like him/her?
    You're feeling that:

6. Inner Child, if you were more like that person what would you be doing differently in your life right now?
    You're feeling that:

7. Inner Child, what teacher did you dislike the most in college (high school, primary school)?
    You're feeling that:

8. Inner Child, why did you dislike him/her so much?
    You're feeling that:

9. Inner Child, where is your favorite place in the whole
    world?
    You're feeling that:

10. Inner Child, what is it about that place that you like so
    much?
    You're feeling that:

11. Inner Child, if you could travel and go anywhere, where
    would you like to go?
    You're feeling that:

12. Inner Child, what would make you feel good going to
    that place?
    You're feeling that:

13. Inner Child, how often would you like to be alone?
    You're feeling that:

14. Inner Child, if you had your choice, would you be alone
    more often or less often? Why?
    You're feeling that:

15. Inner Child, if you had your choice, where would you
    like to go on your next vacation?
    You're feeling that:

16. Inner Child, is there anything else you would like to tell
    me before we end this session?
    You're feeling that:

DAY THIRTEEN

1. Inner Child, how are you feeling right now?
   You're feeling that:

2. Inner Child, are you feeling better physically or emotionally?
   You're feeling that:

3. Inner Child, tell me why you feel that way?
   You're feeling that:

4. Inner Child, what was the best vacation you ever had?
   You're feeling that:

5. Inner Child, why did you like it so much?
   You're feeling that:

6. Inner Child, what was your favorite sexual experience?
   You're feeling that:

7. Inner Child, who was it with?
   You're feeling that:

8. Inner Child, how old were you at the time?
   You're feeling that:

9. Inner Child, what was your worst sexual experience?
    You're feeling that:

10. Inner Child, who was it with?
    You're feeling that:

11. Inner Child, how old were you at the time?
    You're feeling that:

12. Inner Child, can you remember a time when you were successful?
    You're feeling that:

13. Inner Child, tell me more about that time/incident.
    You're feeling that:

14. Inner Child, can you remember a time when you failed?
    You're feeling that:

15. Inner Child, tell me more about that time/incident.
    You're feeling that:

16. Inner Child, is there anything else you would like to tell me before we end this session?
    You're feeling that:

DAY FOURTEEN

1. Inner Child, how are you feeling today?
    You're feeling that:

2. Inner Child, how is your physical body feeling right now?
    You're feeling that:

3. Inner Child, what part of your body feels the most tense?
    You're feeling that:

4. Inner Child, what part of your body feels the most relaxed?
    You're feeling that:

5. Inner Child, what do you remember best about your childhood?
    You're feeling that:

6. Inner Child, why do you remember that?
    You're feeling that:

7. Inner Child, what did you like the least about your childhood?
    You're feeling that:

8. Inner Child, why did you dislike that so much?
    You're feeling that:

9. Inner Child, who were your five favorite school friends? (From college, high school, junior high school, elementary school, kindergarten, preschool?)
   You're feeling that:

10. Inner Child, who do you like spending time with now?
    You're feeling that:

11. Inner Child, why does spending time with that person make you feel good?
    You're feeling that:

12. Inner Child, how often would you like to be alone?
    You're feeling that:

13. Inner Child, if you had your choice, would you be alone more often or less often? Why?
    You're feeling that:

14. Inner Child, do you wish you had more friends?
    You're feeling that:

15. Inner Child, if you had more friends what would they be like?
    You're feeling that:

16. Inner Child, is there anything else you would like to tell me before we end this session?
    You're feeling that:

11

MORE WAYS TO USE THE SELF-PARENTING EXERCISES

INTRODUCTION

The initial purpose of these DAILY half-hour sessions is for you (as the Inner Parent) to learn how to distinguish between the two voices of your Inner Conversations. You ask the questions out loud in the voice of your Inner Parent. **The thoughts and feelings that you hear inside your mind are those of your Inner Child.** Writing down those responses in the proper manner will show your Inner Parent in an objective way the thoughts and feelings of your Inner Child. Thanking the Inner Child after each question completes the cycle, and ending the Self-Parenting session after a half-hour concludes the process.

Amazing progress in the conscious awareness of your Inner Conversations can be made during Self-Parenting sessions. First there is a period of one to two weeks in which you, as the Inner Parent, must come to recognize and know the voice of your Inner Child. As your Self-Parenting sessions deepen and the techniques and skills of your Inner Parent improve, you will discover many opportunities to improve both the relationship with your Inner Child and your life circumstances.

As your Self-Parenting sessions continue you will discover many problems that you (as the Inner Parent) thought you had resolved but which still remain outstanding as Inner Conflicts within your Inner Conversations. Deeper and more powerful issues which have held you back also will begin to rise to conscious awareness. These are problems which have resulted from being unaware of or ignoring your Inner Child until now.

Half-hour sessions are the key to working with your Inner Conversations. Without them there is too much potential for your Inner Parent to revert to Win/Lose parenting during the day. Once basic understanding exists between the two Selves, the Self-Parenting sessions will become a way of working out problems and evolving decisions for your future. They will be the most powerful thirty minutes in your life.

Self-Parenting sessions and awareness of your Inner Conversations can be of practical use in many ways. You can use your half-hour sessions to resolve Inner Conflicts, love, support, and nurture your Inner Child, build your self-esteem, establish or increase motivation for goals, and continue with your question-and-answer sessions.

RESOLVING INNER CONFLICTS

Many times during the day a problem will arise that triggers a major Inner Conflict. Whenever you are confused or can't make a decision, an Inner Conflict exists between your Inner Parent and Inner Child. It may not even be a conflict as much as a misunderstanding or miscommunication between the two Selves. With the pace of modern life being what it is, you may not have time to sit down, write out the Inner Conversation, and positively Self-Parent the situation using the eight steps. You may have to react and make a decision before you have time to consider all the feelings of both Selves.

The perfect time to resolve these situations is during your Self-Parenting sessions. If a problem or Inner Conflict arises during the day, tell your Inner Child that you will work out a solution during your next half-hour session. As a result, your Inner Child will temporarily feel better. But be sure and follow up if you make this promise. If you don't follow through when you say you will, your Inner Child will feel betrayed and it may refuse to believe you the next time you tell it something.

During your next Self-Parenting session, take ten minutes to write out the Inner Conflict and individually list the needs of each Self on your Inner Conversation Dialogue Sheet. Each Inner Self will have its own set of needs and requirements. Spend the next twenty minutes following the eight steps of conflict resolution. Use Win/Win problem-solving to positively Self-Parent the needs of both Inner Parent and Inner Child. Follow the eight steps until **both** sides are satisfied.

LOVING, SUPPORTING, AND NURTURING YOUR INNER CHILD

Sometimes a situation or incident may really upset your Inner Child but due to the outer circumstances you are unable to nurture your Inner Child properly. Rather than an Inner Conflict, this situation is experienced more as a trauma for your Inner Child. When this happened before you became aware of Self-Parenting, you would normally gloss over, ignore, or negate the hurt feelings of your Inner Child in the same way your parents would gloss over, ignore, or negate your hurt feelings as a child.

To end this cycle of abuse you can acknowledge the upset feelings of your Inner Child and promise to take up the situation during your next Self-Parenting session. When something upsets you during the day, use part of your daily half-hour session to soothe the feelings of the Inner Child and explain the reasons why the experience happened or the choices were made. As you begin to follow up on your promises, your Inner Child will learn to depend on your sincerity and concern. It will feel loved, supported, and nurtured in a way it has never felt before!

Use your daily Self-Parenting sessions to work out Inner Conflicts or daily traumas that otherwise would accumulate. Your half-hour sessions are an ideal opportunity for using the Inner Conversation Dialogue Sheet on a regular basis to settle nagging questions, pressing problems, doubts, or indecision. By writing down both sides of your Inner Conversations, you will be able to objectively determine which Self is saying what and what the needs of each Self are. Many times this Self-Parenting step alone will solve or soothe the situation!

Another aspect of loving, supporting, and nurturing yourself is to validate your Inner Child for the little things. For someone with an intense and difficult life, sometimes just putting the cap back on the toothpaste represents a major victory. For some, getting up thirty minutes earlier to do Self-Parenting sessions can become the emotional equivalent of getting engaged.

One student chose to drive to work along a different route at the suggestion of her Inner Child. Even though the trip took a bit longer, her Inner Child was much happier and even her Inner Parent agreed the prettier route was a much more pleasant way to start the day. This person's simple validation of her Inner Child made a big difference in the way she felt all day long.

Another student was going into the kitchen to start morning tea before crawling back into bed to do her half-hour sessions. One day, when she asked her Inner Child if it was comfortable, it complained about having cold feet. Only when she put her slippers on did she realize how cold the floor was, how cold her feet had been, and that she had been uncomfortable during her sessions as a result. As she later said, "It was such an easy solution to a problem I didn't even know I had!"

You will discover many opportunities to love, support, and nurture your Inner Child during the day if you will only pay attention. A basic rule to go by is to give your Inner Child whatever it wants, if it doesn't hurt anyone else (including the Inner Parent). This is especially true of the day-to-day things that we usually take for granted, such as the kind of toothpaste we use or which soap to buy. Your Inner Child has its own opinions and the positive feelings it gives back to you when it is recognized and nurtured will be very rewarding.

BUILDING SELF-ESTEEM

Self-esteem is the opinion your Inner Parent has about your Inner Child and the feelings your Inner Child has about that opinion. Your Inner Child's feelings of esteem result from the quantity and quality of messages your Inner Parent sends during the day. If you consciously tell your Inner Child that you love it five times a day but you tell it unconsciously within your Inner Conversations it is "dumb," "fat," "hopeless," or an "idiot," a hundred times a day, your overall self-esteem will be low.

You must become consciously aware of the language your Inner Parent now uses unconsciously during daily communication with your Inner Child. You may blame, scold, lecture, command, criticize, judge, or threaten your Inner Child many times a day without being aware of the psychological damage you are causing yourself. This behavior is extremely harmful to your self-esteem and is entirely self-inflicted.

The first action step of positive Self-Parenting is to stop criticizing your Inner Child in your Inner Conversations. By doing your Self-Parenting Exercises in the prescribed manner you will automatically have begun this all important step during your half-hour sessions.

The next step is not using negative language with your Inner Child during other activities. To enjoy high levels of self-esteem, your Inner Parent must stop negatively Self-Parenting your Inner Child all the time. Stop giving your Inner Child damaging comments, observations, and opinions during the day. This practice alone gives your Inner

Child a measure of autonomy, respect, acceptance, and control. Stopping negative comments will provide your Inner Child convincing proof of your determination to love, support, and nurture him or her.

The final step is to start giving your Inner Child positive Self-Parenting during your half-hour sessions. Having established a daily positive and nurturing interaction with your Inner Child through the first two weeks' questions, the Inner Parent can now start building self-esteem through the use of positive programming. These sessions will start by reading the standard introduction. Then, instead of asking questions, tell your Inner Child positive things such as:

Inner Child, I care about you.
Inner Child, I want you to be happy.
Inner Child, I appreciate you.
Inner Child, I want you to get what you need and want.
Inner Child, I love you.
Inner Child, you are my favorite person in the whole world.
Inner Child, I love being with you.
Inner Child, you are a treasure.
Inner Child, you are fascinating, brilliant, and beautiful.
Inner Child, you are sexy and desirable.
Inner Child, you are the center of my universe.

As you make these positive Self-Parenting statements to your Inner Child you may get several reactions. One reaction could be disbelief or resistance from the Inner Child. If you experience this type of reaction be sure and write down the negative emotions of your Inner Child using the **"You're feeling that"** formula. Let your Inner Child tell you how and what it feels, thinks, or believes by using the **"You're feeling**

that" formula for every response. Demonstrate to him or her that it is okay to feel and express negative emotions.

After the Inner Child vents its emotions, repeat the positive programming of "I love you" and wait for more responses. As you alternate the positive programming of the Inner Parent with writing down the negative responses of the Inner Child, the disbelief of your Inner Child will gradually soften and let go. Don't let your Self-Parenting session deteriorate into a two-way argument about whether you, the Inner Parent, love the Inner Child or not, or the session becomes unproductive.

It may take several minutes or even several Self-Parenting sessions for your Inner Child to accept positive programmings from your Inner Parent, especially if your initial outer parental programming has been extremely harsh and negative. But even the most resistant Inner Child will come around with persistent practice.

Remember never to judge or criticize your Inner Child during the half-hour sessions. If you tell your Inner Child "I love you" and it responds by saying "No you don't, you never did, you never let me...," your **only** response as the Inner Parent should be **"You're feeling that** no I don't," and **"You're feeling that** I never did," and **"You're feeling that** I never let you." As the Inner Parent, you must allow your Inner Child to fully express whatever it strongly and actually feels.

If your Self-Parenting is naturally nurturing you will feel a very positive emotional response emanating from your Inner Child during this process. Your feelings can range from warm feelings of satisfaction or love to intense and overwhelming sensations of ecstasy or bliss. Again I caution you not to extend these exercises too long. Your best results come through a daily half-hour dose of caring and nurturing from Inner Parent to Inner Child.

Be careful when Self-Parenting **not** to use positive programming in the way affirmations are normally used. The typical affirmation process uses arbitrary programming chosen by the Inner Parent which the Inner Child doesn't feel. The Inner Parent demands acceptance of the positive programming by using repetition and will power.. While the affirmation may "work" for the Inner Parent, the Inner Child is forced to obey. This type of Self-Parenting is a Win/Lose solution which ultimately backfires. The spunk and resistance of your Inner Child will eventually cause rebellion, noncompliance, or other problems.

Many Self-Parenting students have tried using affirmations with little or no lasting success because they did not understand the crucial necessity of the Inner Parent and Inner Child working together. When they changed their Self-Parenting to a more loving, supporting, and nurturing process—after first getting to intimately know and understand their Inner Child—they had much better and more lasting success with their affirmations. Trying to install positive programming over the resistance of the Inner Child creates Win/Lose situations.

All steps for permanent consciousness growth must include Win/Win solutions for both Selves. The Inner Parent can't unilaterally decide that it wants to be happy, rich, and successful today and force the Inner Child to go along, just as an outer parent can't tell an outer child it's going to be happy, rich, and successful and suddenly it happens. One-way actions or demands won't last because cooperation is needed from both sides of the relationship. Both Selves must actively desire the changes for them to become permanent.

The truly positive Inner Parent sends highly charged signals demonstrating an active desire to meet the needs of its Inner Child. **These needs are the ones the Inner Child**

expresses, not the "advice" the negative Inner Parent says the Inner Child "should" take. Tell your Inner Child openly that you want its needs to be met. Encourage your Inner Child to tell you what its needs are so that you, the Inner Parent, can help meet those needs. Supply your Inner Child with many positive assurances that you will give it anything it wants to the best of your ability. The sky is the limit!

ESTABLISHING OR MOTIVATING FOR GOALS

One responsibility of your Inner Parent is to establish worthwhile and positive goals to enhance your life. But your Inner Parent must account for and allow the desires of your Inner Child to be part of the decision making. Based on intellectual knowledge and foresight, your Inner Parent may decide to go to college, change jobs, move to a different city or country, end a relationship, try a different diet, quit smoking, or plan other major life decisions.

Yet the Inner Child must have a say as well. If your Inner Child does not provide energy and enthusiasm, the proposed changes will fail. If your Inner Parent chooses a career your Inner Child hates, you will have a difficult time being a success in that career. If you choose (or actually co-choose) a career that your Inner Child loves, then you will have endless enthusiasm and energy to succeed even if your Inner Parent is intellectually or technically unprepared for that field.

The Inner Parent can always acquire new skills if the Inner Child has a true desire to learn them. It is very difficult for an Inner Parent to manufacture enthusiasm and drive for learning new skills if your Inner Child is uninterested. If the Inner Child is not pleased with the direction your life is going it will rebel, resist, or give up. You will find that most individuals with successful careers have naturally followed the voice of their Inner Child and truly enjoy their work.

If you want to make a lasting improvement in your life in any area, in any way, you must enlist the cooperation of both Selves working together towards your common goals.

The key in this situation is to dialogue and resolve during your Self-Parenting sessions any and all Inner Conflicts that may be generated by the proposed changes. This guarantees the unique strengths and skills of both Selves will be used for the attainment of your goals.

CONTINUING QUESTION-AND-ANSWER SESSIONS

Further questioning of the Inner Child in your Self-Parenting sessions can always be used, as this actively facilitates openness and communication between the two Inner Selves. Your Inner Parent can create questions to ask your Inner Child about current situations in your life or about your past experiences. Or, you can obtain a book of psychological questions and follow them using the **"Inner Child, ..."** format. Half-hour question-and-answer sessions can have the same pleasant aftereffects as an intimate discussion or phone conversation with your best friend.

At other times, getting information of a specific nature from your Inner Child is a mandatory part of solving an Inner Conflict or resolving an outer problem. In these cases you will ask direct questions to your Inner Child expecting an answer in return.

Generic questions can be very useful for this purpose. One dependable example is:

"Inner Child, on a scale of 1–10, how much do you want to _____?"

This question works excellently to presage your Inner Child's interest in a future activity. Does you Inner Child want to go to the mountains or the beach? At 9:00 p.m. on Friday, does it want to watch the television show on channel four or channel two? Would it rather go to a movie or a concert? Is it hungry for something sweet, something salty, or is it really thirsty? By asking your Inner Child using the

1–10 scale, you can tell exactly what priority your Inner Child has and make your decision accordingly.

Another good way to use the 1-10 scale is to ask your Inner Child a question in the following way:

"Inner Child, on a scale of 1-10, how _____ do you feel?"

> **(bored)**
> **(angry)**
> **(unhappy)**
> **(glad)**
> **(rested)**
> **(hungry)**
> **(tired)**

Your Inner Child will immediately give you an answer, or its lack of an answer will tell you that it just doesn't care.

In general, it is better to ask your Inner Child questions which give it a choice between two or three answers, rather that asking it to "fill in the blank." It is easy for an outer child to choose between chocolate, vanilla, or strawberry. If you ask the more general question, "What kind of ice cream do you want?", it then has to choose between thirty-one flavors. Worse yet, if you ask, "What would you like for dessert?", the choices become infinite and the decision or opinion could drag out "forever," as any parent will attest. Asking questions and receiving answers from your Inner Child works in the same manner.

If you do need to ask your Inner Child a direct question, it is best to ask one that gets right to the heart of the matter. The best choices to flesh out your Inner Child's opinion or solve a dilemma are:

"Inner Child, if you had your choice what would you like to do?"

Or:

"Inner Child, what are you feeling?"

Or:

"Inner Child, what is your need?"

The answers popping up in your mind are the opinions of your Inner Child.

WEEK THREE AND FOLLOWING WEEKS

Use your Self-Parenting sessions in one of the following ways.

1. Resolve Inner Conflicts in your life.

2. Love, support, and nurture your Inner Child.

3. Build your self-esteem.

4. Establish and motivate for goals.

5. Continue question and answer sessions with your Inner Child.

12 SELF-PARENTING: FINAL NOTES

SELF-PARENTING YOUR INNER CONVERSATIONS IN THE "REAL WORLD"

As you proceed with your thirty minutes of daily, concentrated Self-Parenting Exercises, you will start hearing more and more of your Inner Conversations throughout the day. Although your Inner Conversations have been continual, you will now become much more aware of them. When this happens don't squelch your Inner Child. Listen to it and respond appropriately.

As a result of your Self-Parenting sessions, your Inner Child will be much more inclined to speak up and voice an opinion or idea during other activities. This is similar to an outer child making a comment or volunteering an observation while walking along with its mother. As you pass a display window in a department store, all of a sudden your Inner Child might say, "_____." And what is your response?

Observing this situation in outer parent/child relationships in supermarkets or bookstores, you have watched parents respond to such comments with behavior ranging from a pleasant acknowledgment or comment, to ignoring, screaming, or slapping the child. Do you Self-Parent your own Inner Child in a like manner several times a day?

Just as in outer parenting, the Inner Parent needs to let the Inner Child grow and express its needs, feelings, and thoughts, no matter how absurd or unrealistic they may be. This is the way your Inner Child grows. As the Inner Child matures in understanding it will also mature in ability. The result will be a much stronger ally in support of you, the Inner Parent, and your outer needs in the "real world."

Any time you hear your Inner Parent giving your Inner Child a hard time (and you will) **STOP IT.** You will get nowhere abusing your Inner Child. Self-denigration is a Lose/Lose proposition for both Selves. Let your Inner Child become more confident as a result of your Self-Parenting sessions. Listen and enjoy your Inner Child becoming more spunky and feisty when you unconsciously ignore or abuse it during the day.

The best way to handle the spontaneous comments and observations of your Inner Child in your daily life is to give your Inner Parent something to do. This "something to do" is to mentally (or even out loud!) feed back the thoughts or impressions you get from your Inner Child. Simply follow the same rules of nonintervention as used during the Self-Parenting sessions. Repeat back the thoughts of your Inner Child using the **"You're feeling that"** technique.

Other situations could arise. Suppose you smell something during the day and it triggers your Inner Child but you can't remember exactly why. Ask your Inner Child for the reason by saying, "Inner Child, what does that remind you of?" When it responds have a conversation with your Inner Child just like you would with your best friend. If you make an excellent squeeze into a tight parking space, thank your Inner Child for doing such a good job. You will have many opportunities to actively and *consciously* engage in Inner Conversations with your Inner Child throughout the day.

SOURCES FOR FURTHER STUDY

As you have learned, you need to actually Self-Parent your Inner Child. It is not enough to know that Self-Parenting exists (Level One understanding). You must also learn to use this knowledge as therapy (Level Two and Three Understanding) to make yourself feel better. You can use the Self-Parenting Exercises to heal and love yourself whenever you feel depressed, fearful, out of sorts, or angry. You can use your daily half-hour sessions to fix yourself up when you are really down through loving, supporting, and nurturing your Inner Child.

For further study in Self-Parenting, I recommend the following books. Each one in its own way gives valuable insight to the "Inner" process of Self-Parenting. By reading these texts, using the newfound awareness of your Inner Conversations, and following through with consistent and positive Self-Parenting sessions, you can work out your ideal Self-Parenting style and practice living by it where it really counts, within your Inner Conversations.

Reading these books will be another way for your Inner Parent to become consciously aware of the unconscious methods you use to Self-Parent. These books must be read with the awareness of Self-Parenting within your Inner Conversations to have their greatest effect. Even if you have previously read one or more of these books you will want to read them again, calling to mind the principles of Self-Parenting. My comments on each book are directed to this understanding and are an unsolicited testimonial to these authors. All of these books are available at or can be ordered through your local bookstore.

P.E.T. — Parent Effectiveness Training

Thomas Gordon. New York: New American Library, 1975

This book is a masterpiece of successful outer parenting methods. We all owe a debt to Thomas Gordon for making the concepts of outer parenting so easy to understand. Use the methods of active listening with your Inner Child. The section on the "twelve roadblocks" is especially enlightening as it shows the multiple ways that you, as the Inner Parent, can roadblock your Inner Child. This is the next book you must read (or reread) to develop Self-Parenting skills.

Your Inner Child of the Past

Hugh Missildine, M.D. New York: Simon & Shuster, 1963

The first book I know of that discusses the "Inner Child" in a major way. It is especially valuable as it documents how the type of parenting you received as an outer child creates the response behavior style of your Inner Child.

Your Baby and Child — From Birth To Age Five

Penelope Leach. New York: Viking Penguin Inc., 1977

Another brilliant book about outer child rearing. While reading this book I saw so many applications of her methods and understanding of raising a baby/child to Self-Parenting I was amazed. Use this book to develop your awareness as an Inner Parent, especially in the areas of loving and spoiling, feeding, everyday care, sleeping, and comforting. The pictures alone will trigger emotional responses from your Inner Child.

Inner Skiing

Timothy Gallwey & Bob Kriegel. New York: Bantam Books, 1977

This book reflects a classic and intuitive understanding of Inner Conversation dynamics, Self One being the Inner

Parent and Self Two being the Inner Child. Using concrete examples from sports, the authors demonstrate how a positive, understanding Inner Parent can consciously Self-Parent the Inner Child to achieve increased performance without destroying the relationship between the two. Must reading. Also recommended are any other books by the same authors.

Diets Don't Work
Bob Schwartz. Oakland, CA: Breakthru Publishing, 1982

Many of you are struggling with diet problems that are symptomatic of deep and longstanding Inner Conflicts between your Inner Parent and Inner Child. Weight problems are an advanced issue of Self-Parenting. I wouldn't recommend tackling them until you have done your Self-Parenting sessions for at least three months, especially the self-esteem processes, and have read the other recommended books. When you do want to tackle them use Bob Schwartz's advanced understanding of dieting dynamics along with the principles of Self-Parenting and you will do well.

Handbook to Higher Consciousness
Ken Keyes. Coos Bay, OR: Living Love Publications, 1975

This book, also a classic, should be read to educate your Inner Parent. Although the principles in this book are intellectually flawless, they are most suited for stopping the specific type of mental negativity the Inner Parent creates. In my opinion "The Methods" do not translate well towards the emotional concepts of loving, supporting, and nurturing the Inner Child within your Inner Conversations. In other words, use "The Methods" described in the book to educate your Inner Parent, not overpower or invalidate the emotions of your Inner Child.

Making Peace With Your Parents
Harold Bloomfield, M.D. New York: Ballantine Books, 1983

An excellent treatise on reestablishing the bonds with parental figures to facilitate and enhance your own Self-Parenting. Dr. Bloomfield covers a variety of concepts.

Feeling Good: The New Mood Therapy
David D. Burns, M.D. New York: New American Library, 1980

Another excellent text for the Inner Parent. Has many examples of helpful techniques to get the Inner Parent off the Inner Child's back. This book shows how "Cognitive Distortions," or (Inner Parent) erroneous thinking, can make life miserable.

Wishcraft: How to Get What You Really Want
Barbara Sher. New York: Ballantine Books, 1979

Possibly the most helpful book I've ever read! An amazing analysis of the step-by-step process for achieving anything you want in life. *Wishcraft* combined with *Self-Parenting* presents an unbeatable combination. No more excuses for not knowing what you want or not being able to get it. *Self-Parenting* unveils the buried treasure of what you truly want and need, and *Wishcraft* provides the directions and the map. You do the rest. This book also demonstrates incredibly intuitive support for the needs of the Inner Child.

FURTHER SOURCES OF PROFESSIONAL REFERRAL

The harsher your outer parenting as a child, the harsher your Self-Parenting will be as an Inner Parent. The most damaging outer parenting by far seems to be that given to the children of alcoholic parents. The coping mechanisms and defense patterns required by these children for survival are equivalent to those needed by concentration camp survivors. These patterns and issues are extremely deep and very difficult to overcome by oneself due to the nature of self-denial and self-isolation required for survival by the victims.

One out of three families in America currently reports alcohol abuse by a family member. If one, or especially both, of your parents was consistently impaired during your childhood years by alcohol or other drugs, it is recommended that you seek intervention through a therapist or organization that expressly understands and is trained to recognize the psychological issues of the adult child of an alcoholic. Self-Parenting under these circumstances is simply too difficult and exhausting to undertake on your own.

People who have suffered severe outer parenting will have trouble easily putting the concepts of Self-Parenting to practical use, If either of your parents were heavy drinkers, you might not even be aware that you've had this type of problem parenting due to the special nature of denial involved. Two books to help you understand these deeper issues of Self-Parenting are:

Guide to Recovery: A Book for Children of Alcoholics
Herbert L. Gravitz & Julie C. Bowden. Holmes Beach, FL: Learning Publications, 1985

Adult Children of Alcoholics
Janet Woititz. Pompano Beach, FL: Health Communications, 1983

Two organizations that specialize in referring or assisting those with problems concerning Children of Alcoholics are:

National Association for Children of Alcoholics
31706 Coast Highway. Suite 201
South Laguna, CA 92677
(714) 499-3889

Adult Children of Alcoholics
Post Office Box 35623
Los Angeles, CA 90035
(213) 464-4423

CONCLUSION

The parent/child relationship is the primary relationship of humanity. Each of us began life within the cocoon of our mother's womb. Each of us was programmed for better or for worse by parents that did the best they could given their set of circumstances. What your parents did or didn't do while parenting you is now of lesser consequence. What matters today is how you perpetuate within your Inner Conversations the parenting dynamics they transferred to you.

The relationship dynamics discovered in your Inner Conversations are those that exist in all parent/child relationships. The dynamics of these two roles must be manifested, each side exhibiting their classic strengths. Perhaps this seems obvious to you now. What may not be so obvious is how successful your life can become when you train yourself to become a better Inner Parent by consciously studying the successful methods of outer parenting.

Develop the ability to give yourself a profound healing experience. Have your Inner Parent cuddle your Inner Child when it is crying. Use the technique of **"Your feeling that..."** when your Inner Child is under emotional stress. Use the Self-Parenting Exercises and awareness of your Inner Conversations to give yourself a sense of being nurtured and of meeting your own needs rather than waiting for others to provide them. Ultimately you can heal yourself completely, no matter how old the wounds may be.

I hope my sharing of the ideas contained in this book has motivated and stimulated you to provide happiness, meaning, and fulfillment for both your Inner Parent and your Inner Child. You will discover many Inner Truths once the awareness and power of these Self-Parenting concepts have become part of you; we are only now beginning to understand their potential. You have discovered the secret of **your** universe: Self-Parenting within **your** Inner Conversations.

DR. JOHN POLLARD has researched and developed consciousness growth concepts since 1969 and is an expert on Self-Parenting and resolving Inner Conflicts. His Self-Parenting Program is taught in major cities throughout the U.S. and is the only one of its kind. Self-Parenting represents a quantum leap in consciousness growth awareness and Dr. Pollard's warm, personable, yet direct style has influenced thousands towards becoming healthier, saner human beings.

LINDA NUSBAUM is a freelance painter, designer, and illustrator. A graduate of the Otis Art Institute of Parson's School of Design, she works on a variety of projects on both coasts, including interactive exhibits for children's museums, film storyboards, murals, and oil paintings. She lives in Los Angeles with her husband.

Generic Human Studies Publishing

Generic Human Studies defines a new standard concerning human consciousness potential. To study human potential there is no need for exclusionary policies, cultist ideas, or groups that claim "exclusive knowledge." Each generic human communicates, is in relationships, desires happiness, wants to be healthy, and requires financial independence. Why make the study of human potential more difficult or expensive than need be?

Generic Human Studies Publishing supports the condensation of the diverse and unique insights of different researchers into what they are—generic knowledge concerning the different aspects of the five human meta-functions: Human Communication, Human Relationships, Human Happiness, Human Health, and Human Financial Independence.

We are all human beings; we all have common needs. It is time for each person, group, and nation to face this reality and start helping each other to grow through meeting our common needs.

Once the personal needs of one individual become fulfilled, it is a natural extension for him or her to help other humans meet their needs. As a result, fulfilled and happy groups of humans can help other unfulfilled and unhappy people to improve their experience of life. A successful development from the study of GHS philosophy, science, and art would be more individuals, groups, and nations carrying their own weight in life by not consuming the resources and energies of others without contributing in return.

For a recommended reading list on specific human meta-functions, please send a stamped, self-addressed #10 (business-size) envelope to:

Generic Human Studies Publishing
P.O. Box 6466, Malibu, CA 90265
Attention: Recommended Reading List

A Gift for You
$15

To be applied toward tuition for any
Self-Parenting Program Seminar

Signature_____

YES! Please contact me with more information about:

☐ Self-Parenting Program Seminar

☐ Quantity discounts on *Self-Parenting* book

☐ Having Dr. Pollard speak at my convention or
meeting

☐ Help with starting a Self-Parenting support group in
my own area

Name_____

Address_____

City_____ State_____ Zip_____

Home Phone _____ Work Phone_____

Acceptable as payment along with deposit as

registration for any Self-Parenting

Program Seminar.

To redeem this gift certificate call

(213) 457-1140

or detach and mail the information

postcard below.

Mail to:

Self-Parenting Program Seminar
P.O. Box 6535
Malibu, CA. 90265